5-
1995

Ernest Hemingway's
THE SUN ALSO RISES

Bloom's
NOTES

A CONTEMPORARY
LITERARY VIEWS BOOK

Edited and with an Introduction by
HAROLD BLOOM

© 1996 by Chelsea House Publishers, a division of Main Line Book Co.

Introduction © 1996 by Harold Bloom

Printed and bound in the United States of America.

First Printing
1 3 5 7 9 8 6 4 2

Cover illustration: Photofest

Library of Congress Cataloging-in-Publication Data

Ernest Hemingway's The sun also rises / edited and with an introduction by Harold Bloom.
p.   cm. — (Bloom's Notes)
Includes bibliographical references (p.) and index.
Summary: Includes a brief biography of the author, thematic and structural analysis of the work, critical views, and an index of themes and ideas.
ISBN 0-7910-4075-5
1. Hemingway, Ernest, 1899–1961. Sun also rises. [1. Hemingway, Ernest, 1899–1961. Sun also rises. 2. American literature—History and criticism.] I. Bloom, Harold. II. Series.
PS3515.E37S8 1996
813'.52—dc20
95-43493
CIP
AC

Chelsea House Publishers
1974 Sproul Road, Suite 400
P.O. Box 914
Broomall, PA 19008-0914

Contents

User's Guide

This volume is designed to present biographical, critical, and bibliographical information on Ernest Hemingway and *The Sun Also Rises*. Following Harold Bloom's introduction, there appears a detailed biography of the author, discussing the major events in his life and his important literary works. Then follows a thematic and structural analysis of the work, in which significant themes, patterns, and motifs are traced. An annotated list of characters supplies brief information on the chief characters in the work.

A selection of critical extracts, derived from previously published material by leading critics, then follows. The extracts consist of statements by the author on his work, early reviews of the work, and later evaluations down to the present day. The items are arranged chronologically by date of first publication. A bibliography of Hemingway's writings (including a complete listing of all books he wrote, cowrote, edited, and translated, and selected posthumous publications), a list of additional books and articles on him and on *The Sun Also Rises,* and an index of themes and ideas conclude the volume.

Harold Bloom is Sterling Professor of the Humanities at Yale University and Henry W. and Albert A. Berg Professor of English at the New York University Graduate School. He is the author of twenty books and the editor of more than thirty anthologies of literature and literary criticism.

Professor Bloom's works include *Shelley's Mythmaking* (1959), *The Visionary Company* (1961), *Blake's Apocalypse* (1963), *Yeats* (1970), *A Map of Misreading* (1975), *Kabbalah and Criticism* (1975), and *Agon: Towards a Theory of Revisionism* (1982). *The Anxiety of Influence* (1973) sets forth Professor Bloom's provocative theory of the literary relationships between the great writers and their predecessors. His most recent books are *The American Religion* (1992) and *The Western Canon* (1994).

Professor Bloom earned his Ph.D. from Yale University in 1955 and has served on the Yale faculty since then. He is a 1985 MacArthur Foundation Award recipient and served as the Charles Eliot Norton Professor of Poetry at Harvard University in 1987–88. He is currently the editor of the Chelsea House series Major Literary Characters and Modern Critical Views, and other Chelsea House series in literary criticism.

Introduction

HAROLD BLOOM

So severely stylized and rigorously mannered is Ernest Hemingway's *The Sun Also Rises* that it continues to achieve a classic status, seven decades after its initial publication. It is a masterpiece of stance and of sensibility, and like *The Great Gatsby* (which influenced it) *The Sun Also Rises* evades all the dangers that might have reduced it to become another mere period piece. Again like *The Great Gatsby, The Sun Also Rises* is something of a prose-poem, emerging from the literary era dominated by T. S. Eliot's *The Waste Land*. Like Eliot himself, who was much affected by Joseph Conrad's *Heart of Darkness*, both Fitzgerald and Hemingway take up a narrative stance that is influenced by Conrad's Marlow, the prime narrator of *Heart of Darkness, Lord Jim,* and (though he is unnamed there) "The Secret Sharer." Nick Carraway in *The Great Gatsby* and Jake Barnes in *The Sun Also Rises* are equivocal narrators, each with a protagonist who is his main concern: Gatsby for Carraway, and Lady Brett Ashley for Jake Barnes. There is something feminine in sensibility about both Carraway and Barnes, as there was about Conrad's Marlow, and about Eliot's Tiresias, the implied narrative sensibility of *The Waste Land*.

The wounded Fisher King of *The Waste Land,* impotent and yearning for spiritual salvation, is clearly akin to the impotent Jake Barnes, maimed in World War I and so no longer Brett Ashley's lover, though they continue to be in love with one another. Interpreters of Brett take remarkably varied views of her, ranging from a man-eating, Circean bitch-goddess to another lost Waste Lander, stoic and disinterested and essentially tragic, questing for what cannot be recovered, a lost image of sexual fulfillment. It is suggestive that the hidden model for Eliot's *The Waste Land* was the most powerful of all American poems, Walt Whitman's elegy for the martyred Abraham Lincoln, *When Lilacs Last in the Dooryard Bloom'd.* Whitman's poem is truly a self-elegy, as are *The Waste Land, The Great Gatsby,* and *The Sun Also Rises.* When the funeral procession of President Lincoln passes him, Whitman makes a symbolic gesture of self-castration by surrendering the "tally," the sprig of lilac that was his own image of voice, and more ambiguously the image for his sexual identity. Elegy is the literary genre of *The Sun Also Rises* and ought to help determine our attitude towards Brett as well as towards Jake, who mourns not only his lost potency but his largely abandoned Catholicism.

Hemingway's nostalgias were numerous: for God, heroism, a perfect love, and an antagonistic supremacy in Western literature, even against such titans as Melville and Tolstoy. *The Sun Also Rises* profoundly studies many other American nostalgias but above all our longing for innocence, in the Whitmanian sense of an original American destiny, compounded of freedom, hope, and millennial potential. Against that "optative mood," as Ralph Waldo Emerson termed it, Hemingway sets the negativity of Ecclesiastes, the most nihilistic book of the Hebrew Bible. The novel's epigraph, the source of its title, states Hemingway's ethos and also the stoic condition of Jake Barnes and Brett Ashley:

> One generation passeth away, and another generation cometh; but the earth abideth forever. . . . The sun also ariseth, and the sun goeth down, and hasteth to the place where he arose. . . . The wind goeth toward the south, and turneth about unto the north; it whirleth about continually, and the wind returneth again according to his circuits. . . . All the rivers run into the sea; yet the sea is not full; unto the place from whence the rivers come, thither they return again.

All the generations are lost—not just that of Brett and Jake and their friends—in this dark view of mortality and mutability. *The Sun Also Rises,* like Ecclesiastes, does not urge us either to religious assurance or to an absolute nihilism or despair. One of the most poignant of all American elegies, it affirms the virtues of giving a style to despair and of enduring the loss of love with something like a tragic dignity. Hemingway was never again to write so compelling a novel, though his genius for the short story continued undiminished. Lyrical intensity has rarely sustained a novel with such economy, or such grace. ❖

Biography of Ernest Hemingway

Ernest Hemingway was born on July 21, 1899, to Dr. Clarence and Mrs. Grace Hall Hemingway in Oak Park, Illinois. Clarence Hemingway, an avid hunter and fisherman, shared his love of the outdoors with his son each summer at Walloon Lake in northern Michigan, which influenced many of his stories. During the rest of the year, Hemingway attended public school in Oak Park, where he actively participated in athletics and wrote columns in the style of sportswriter Ring Lardner for the school newspaper.

When he graduated from high school in 1917, he skipped college to pursue journalism. For seven months, Hemingway received a valuable on-the-job education as a cub reporter at the Kansas City *Star* but longed to join the American troops overseas fighting World War I. Rejected by the army because of an eye injury, he became an ambulance driver for the Red Cross. In July 1918, he was seriously injured by shrapnel near Fossalta di Piave, Italy, and was decorated by the Italians for his bravery. After recuperating in Milan, he returned to Michigan in January 1919.

Bored with inactivity, Hemingway soon began writing features for the Toronto *Star.* In 1920, he also worked as a contributing editor of a trade journal in Chicago, where he met Hadley Richardson. The couple married a year later and moved to France. Hemingway traveled through Europe as a foreign correspondent for the Toronto *Star* and spent much time in Paris associating with expatriate American writers such as Gertrude Stein and Ezra Pound. After a brief return to Toronto for the birth of his first son, he quit the *Star* and settled in Paris to become a literary writer.

He published two small volumes of prose and poetry in Paris but did not receive attention in the United States until the 1925 publication of *In Our Time,* a collection of short stories. The book—which included the first appearance of Nick Adams, a recurring character who is a typically masculine, but sensitive,

"Hemingway hero"—received great critical response for its understated, realistic style. The following year, he published his novel *The Sun Also Rises* to even greater acclaim. With its depiction of the hopelessness of postwar expatriates, the novel became a definitive rendering of the "lost generation."

Having made his name in Paris, the writer sought new places and experiences. In 1927, he divorced his wife, married Pauline Pfeiffer, and set up house in Key West, Florida. The birth of another son and the suicide of his father took him away from his work, but by 1929 he completed his well-received novel *A Farewell to Arms*. Drawn from his World War I experience, the book portrayed a disillusioned American who deserts the Italian army and tragically loses his lover. While Hemingway continued to spend time in Key West deep-sea fishing, after his last son was born in 1931 he increasingly roamed the world looking for adventure and new material. His nonfiction books *Death in the Afternoon* (1932) and *Green Hills of Africa* (1935) deal with his interests in Spanish bullfights and African big-game hunting, respectively.

Renowned as a sportsman, Hemingway also began to express social and political interests in his writing. His 1937 novel, *To Have and Have Not,* concerns a man who becomes an outlaw to feed his family during the Depression. During the Spanish Civil War (1936–39), he acted on his political beliefs by supporting the Loyalist side and reporting as a war correspondent. *The Fifth Column,* his only full-length play, takes place during the siege of Madrid; the work was published in 1938, along with the short stories from his collections *In Our Time, Men without Women* (1927), and *Winner Take Nothing* (1933). Although the play received little notice, the short stories "The Killers," "The Short Happy Life of Francis Macomber," and "The Snows of Kilimanjaro" among others are still widely appreciated. His Spanish war experience also inspired the 1940 novel *For Whom the Bell Tolls,* a less pessimistic tale emphasizing the brotherhood of mankind.

For the next several years, Hemingway was too busy to publish. After divorcing his second wife, he married Martha Gellhorn and bought an estate called La Finca Vigia outside Havana, Cuba. He spent little time there, however, choosing instead to follow the wars then raging around the world. Before the Japanese attack on Pearl Harbor, he reported from China on the Sino-Japanese War. After the United States entered World War II, he became a war correspondent for *Collier's*. In London, he met journalist Mary Welsh, who later became his fourth wife. From there he ventured to France, where he followed American troops through the Battle of the Bulge and the liberation of Paris. Hemingway became something of a legend, joining the fighting as much as reporting about it.

After the war, he returned to his life of writing and traveling. In 1950, he published *Across the River and into the Trees,* a novel about an aging army colonel that is generally considered inferior to the rest of his work. However, his next book, *The Old Man and the Sea* (1952), received the highest accolades, including a Pulitzer Prize. A chronicle of a fisherman's struggle to catch a huge marlin only to lose it to sharks, the book celebrates man's dignity and endurance as a kind of victory despite defeat. Hemingway experienced a major victory of his own in 1954, when he was awarded the Nobel Prize for literature.

Although in the prime of his life, Hemingway's enjoyment was hindered by ill health. Besides two harrowing plane crashes in Africa, he suffered spells of depression and had to be hospitalized twice at the Mayo Clinic. On July 2, 1961, Hemingway used a shotgun to commit suicide at his home in Ketchum, Idaho.

Hemingway left a lasting legacy. In 1964, *A Moveable Feast,* his memories of Paris, was published, and in 1970, the three-part *Islands in the Stream,* a novel about Bimini and Cuba, was released. His novels continue to be widely studied, and his spare, brutal style remains greatly influential. ❖

Thematic and Structural Analysis

Book one of *The Sun Also Rises* begins with the announcement that "Robert Cohn was once middleweight boxing champion of Princeton," although, the narrator quickly adds, he himself is not impressed by this, and even Cohn did not like boxing but took it up to "counteract the feeling of inferiority and shyness he had felt on being treated as a Jew at Princeton" (**chapter one**). The narrator, as yet unidentified, offers the reader a brief account of Cohn's life after college—a life often marked by happenstance and passivity—up to the present, which finds him living rather unhappily as an expatriate writer in Paris with his jealous lover, Frances. The chapter ends with a scene in a restaurant in which the narrator, now identified as "Jake," gets kicked under the table by Frances for suggesting that Cohn meet a woman he knows. Cohn asks Jake not to "get sore" over Frances's possessive behavior, and Jake reflects, "I rather liked him and evidently she led him quite a life." Thus the opening chapter introduces the narrator with his simultaneously sympathetic and critical point of view; and Cohn, one of the novel's chief instigators of conflict.

Chapter two continues Cohn's biography and exhibits some of the anti-Semitism prevalent among Hemingway's expatriate crowd. These sentiments will become more pointed and, as many critics see it, unnecessary as the novel progresses. Jake tells us that while Cohn was in America after the publication of his novel, he enjoyed the attention of several women, which "changed him so that he was not so pleasant to have around." Returning to the present, Jake presents us with a scene where Cohn, telling Jake that he is afraid he is not really living, expresses a naive yet insistent desire to go to South America. Reflecting that Cohn has "a hard Jewish stubborn streak," Jake tries to convince him to enjoy life in Paris, a city Cohn cannot seem to appreciate.

In **chapter three** Hemingway's readers are given a portrait of the dissolute life led by so many expatriate Americans in Paris during the 1920s. We recall the novel's first epigraph—

Gertrude Stein's statement, "You are all a lost generation." We also learn that the novel's narrator, Jake Barnes, was left impotent by an injury during World War I; leaving a café with a prostitute named Georgette, he resists her advances by telling her, "I got hurt in the war." Arriving at a dance club, Jake jokingly introduces Georgette to his friends as his fiancée and then watches as she is taken up by a group of homosexuals who have arrived with Lady Brett Ashley. Cohn asks Brett to dance, but she brushes him off and dances with Jake. The two then leave the club together, and Brett tells Jake, "Oh, darling, I've been so miserable."

Chapter four begins with Jake kissing Brett in a taxi. She begs him not to touch her, even though she confesses that she loves him. They stop at the Café Select, where Jake leaves Brett in the company of Count Mippipopolous, a very rich, fat man who is treating his friends to champagne. Going home alone to his flat, Jake reads his mail, which includes two bullfight papers from Spain. Unable to sleep, he frets about his war wound, "the old grievance." He starts to cry, which makes him feel better, and then sleeps until he is awakened by a row downstairs between the concierge and Brett. Up in his flat, Brett tells Jake that the count has asked her to go away with him but that she has told him she is in love with Jake. Jake declines to go out with Brett and the count for the rest of the night, but agrees to have dinner with them the following evening, and Brett leaves. In Hemingway's deceptively simple language, Jake reflects that "it is awfully easy to be hard-boiled about everything in the daytime, but at night it is another thing."

Chapters five and six show three scenes in restaurants and cafés where conversations go badly for Cohn. Having lunch with Jake, Cohn quizzes him about Brett Ashley, saying, "I shouldn't wonder if I were in love with her." When Jake tells Cohn that Brett is "a drunk" who has twice married men she did not love, Cohn gets angry. Jake tells Cohn to "go to hell," which the immature and idealistic Cohn demands he take back, and Jake carelessly acquiesces. The next chapter shows Cohn in a café taking insults from Jake's drunken and reclusive friend, Harvey Stone. At this point, Jake tells us that he feels he has not depicted Cohn accurately. He reflects that "until he fell in love with Brett, I never heard him make one remark that would, in any way, distinguish him from other people." Jake attempts to list some of Cohn's strong points: good looks, athleticism, amiability. Frances arrives, takes Jake away for a walk, and tells him that Cohn is about to leave her. When the two return to Cohn's table, she vents her frustration in a scathing attack on Cohn that depicts him as a stingy, self-pitying adolescent. Jake leaves them, wondering to himself, "Why did he keep on taking it like that?"

Chapter seven returns to Jake and Brett's doomed relationship. Jake is getting out of the shower when Brett arrives at the flat with the count, who brings Jake a large bunch of roses—a gift that, though meant kindly, underscores Jake's emasculation. Jake is dressing when Brett comes into his room; he tells her he loves her and asks why they cannot live together. Brett says, "I'd just *tromper* you with everybody. You couldn't stand it." Jake's reply to this is, "I stand it now." Brett says she is going away from Jake until her fiancé, Mike, returns, as it will be better for them both. Brett and Jake drink champagne with the count, then go to dinner and out dancing. But during dinner, the count himself asks why Jake and Brett do not get married. She seems happy, but the next moment she is miserable and, being dropped at home by Jake, will not let him come to her room.

In **book two** the characters leave their comfortable but meaningless lives in Paris and head toward the bullfighting in Pamplona, Spain. At the beginning of **chapter eight**, Jake notes that he did not see Brett or Cohn for a few weeks, but that he received a short note from each. He prepares for his holiday, which will be spent with his friend Bill Gorton, a witty character whose wisecracks provide the novel with much of its humor—but also with further elements of racism. As Jake and Bill are walking to a restaurant on the day of Bill's arrival, Brett pulls up in a taxi. She declines dinner, saying she must have a bath before Mike arrives—the first of many references she will make to bathing or cleaning her body. Later that evening, Jake and Bill meet her at the Café Select with her fiancé, Mike Campbell, a bankrupt Scot who is sure to inherit money from his wealthy family. We immediately sense that he can be both drunk and crude when he repeatedly calls Brett "a lovely piece." The chapter ends with Jake's observation that "Mike was pretty excited about his girl friend." "Well," responds Bill, "you can't blame him such a hell of a lot."

Chapter nine sees the formation of the party that will travel to Pamplona—a party immediately revealed as conflicted. For not only does Cohn wire that he would like to accompany Jake and Bill on their fishing trip before going with them to Pamplona for the festival of San Fermin, but Brett and Mike also decide to come along—and, we now learn, it was Cohn whom Brett had just been away with in San Sebastian. Brett writes to Cohn to dissuade him, but is surprised to find that he is "keen" about the trip. All plan to meet in Pamplona, and the rest of the chapter describes Bill and Jake's train ride to Bayonne, during which they are annoyed to find that a large group of American Catholics has monopolized the train's dining cars— Jake particularly annoyed, as he is Catholic himself. The two are met at the train by Cohn, looking nearsighted and shy, who takes them to his hotel.

Jake, Bill, and Cohn spend the morning in Bayonne before traveling by car to Pamplona, where the rest of **chapter ten** takes place. As they check out of their hotel—one chosen by Cohn—they notice a huge cockroach crawling across the floor. "We agreed he must have just come in from the garden," says Jake. "It was really an awfully clean hotel." During the car ride, Jake and Bill admire the scenery, while Cohn falls asleep, thereby demonstrating both his position as an outsider and his inability to appreciate what life has to offer him. Once in Pamplona, the three check into the Hotel Montoya, and Jake notices that Cohn appears nervous. In a superior tone of voice, Cohn tells Jake and Bill that he thinks Brett and Mike will not be coming. This comment irritates them both and leads Bill to make a foolish bet with Cohn. After lunch, Jake goes into the cathedral and prays for Brett, Mike, Bill, Cohn, and the bull-fighters. His mind wanders at the end of his prayer, making him feel sorry that he is such a "rotten Catholic"—further developing another theme in the novel, the elusiveness of an established code of morality.

At dinner, it is evident to Jake that Cohn has been to the barber in his nervous anticipation of Brett's arrival. Cohn even gets up in the middle of the meal to meet the train from San

Sebastian. Jake accompanies him just to "devil" him and enjoys Cohn's nervousness: "It was lousy to enjoy it, but I felt lousy. Cohn had a wonderful quality of bringing out the worst in anybody." Brett and Mike are not on the train, so Jake and Cohn return to the hotel, where Cohn calls off his bet with Bill. Jake then receives a telegram from Brett and Mike, saying that they have stayed the night in San Sebastian—which Jake blithely relays to Cohn. For at this moment he hates Cohn: "I was blind, unforgivably jealous of what had happened to him." Jake and Bill plan to leave for Burguete the next morning to go fishing, but Cohn decides to stay, claiming that Brett and Mike might be expecting him in San Sebastian, which further exasperates the other two.

Chapters eleven and twelve recount Bill and Jake's short fishing excursion to Burguete. As soon as they board the bus, we can see that the trip will offer a respite from the complexities of Cohn and Brett and instead provide simple, elemental pleasures: drinking from the wineskins offered by the Basque peasants on the bus; eating, drinking, and sleeping well at their inn. On the first day of fishing, Jake gets up early to dig worms, while Bill launches into a sequence of wordplays about "irony and pity"—"You're only . . . an expatriated newspaperman. You ought to be ironical the minute you get out of bed. You ought to wake up with your mouth full of pity"—a series of witticisms that loses momentum when he inadvertently makes a remark about impotence. After Jake and Bill catch trout, they engage in another jocular conversation, with Bill making a fetish out of the word *utilize.* But this conversation also ends on a serious note when Jake confesses to Bill that he has been in love with Brett "off and on for a hell of a long time."

The fast-running river, with its abundant trout and narcotic effect on the two men, reminds the reader of a portion of the novel's second epigraph, taken from Ecclesiastes: "All the rivers run into the sea; yet the sea is not full; unto the place from whence the rivers come, thither they return again." At this point of the novel, nature seems harmonious and healing—unlike the inharmonious, downward path into unhappiness that so many of the characters will follow during the festival in Pamplona. For after five days in Burguete, Jake and

Bill receive conflicting telegrams: the first, that Mike and Brett are going straight into Pamplona; the second, that Cohn is coming to meet Jake and Bill in Burguete. They wire Cohn that they are returning to Pamplona.

Arriving at the Hotel Montoya (**chapter thirteen**), Jake and Bill are greeted by Montoya himself, who has a high regard for Jake because of his *aficion* (passion) for the bullfights. Jake explains that just as Montoya will forgive a bullfighter with aficion anything, he also forgives Jake for bringing his friends, people who clearly lack aficion, into his hotel. After speaking to Montoya, Jake explains to Bill how the bulls are unloaded into the corral, where they are received by steers who "run around like old maids trying to quiet them down" and who later are often gored for their efforts. After they meet Cohn, Brett, and Mike at the café, the group goes to watch the bulls being unloaded, and a steer is indeed gored.

Back at the café, Mike attacks Cohn, accusing him of following Brett around like a steer. After Cohn leaves with Bill, Mike says that he knows that Brett has been with other men, "but they weren't ever Jews, and they didn't come and hang about afterward." Bill later tells Jake that although he does not like Cohn, Mike should not have spoken to him as he did. They all meet again at dinner, and Jake notices that just looking at Brett seems to make Cohn happy: "It was like certain dinners I remember from the war. There was much wine, an ignored tension, and a feeling of things coming that you could not prevent happening."

Chapter fourteen begins with Jake lying in bed after dinner, trying to keep the room from spinning by reading. He thinks about his friendship with Brett and how he had been trying to get something for nothing when, according to his own philosophy, "the bill always came. That was one of the swell things you could always count on." Jake muses that he wants to know how to live in the world. He also wishes that Mike would not treat Cohn so badly, even though he enjoys watching Cohn get hurt. But that feeling makes Jake disgusted with himself, reflecting that "that must be morality. Things that made you disgusted afterward." These ruminations stop when Jake returns to his reading.

The rest of the chapter describes the two days before the fiesta—quiet days with "no more rows." On one occasion, Brett accompanies Jake to church, eager to hear him go to confession. After Jake tells her that she will find it disappointing, they leave the church and meet Cohn, who has been following them. The good weather and his good spirits make Jake feel friendly to Cohn. He notes, "That was the last day before the fiesta."

In **chapter fifteen**, the Fiesta of San Fermin "explodes." Sitting with Cohn and Bill at an iron café table installed to withstand the festivities, Jake watches the street dancers: "People were coming into the square from all sides, and down the street we heard the pipes and the fifes and the drums coming." As Cohn leaves the table to find Brett and Mike, Jake ruminates about fiestas and foreshadows coming events: "The things that happened could only have happened during a fiesta. Everything became quite unreal finally and it seemed as though nothing could have any consequences." In the afternoon, the group goes to watch the religious procession, but Brett is refused entry to the church for not wearing a hat, so they return to the streets where a group of dancers, wearing wreathes of garlic around their necks, forms a circle around Brett: "They wanted her as an image to dance around." The dancers push Bill and Jake into the circle and then take them all into a wineshop, where everybody drinks together, with Jake leaving briefly to purchase wineskins. When he returns, he learns that Cohn has passed out from drinking—another sign of his bad timing and general incompatibility with the others.

That night, unable to find his keys, Jake sleeps in Cohn's room and misses going with the others to watch the running of the bulls. Instead, he watches from the balcony. After breakfast, Jake and the rest of the group go to the café, where they are caught up in the general excitement of the fiesta: "The café did not make this same noise at any other time no matter how crowded it was. This hum went on, and we were with it and a part of it."

It is at this point in the novel that Hemingway finally describes the bullfights—the authentic experience Jake has been looking forward to all year during his anesthetized life in

Paris. But before Hemingway describes the actual bullfighting, which he does in some detail, he introduces another conflict between Cohn and the others, as well as a new character: the nineteen-year-old bullfighter Pedro Romero. As the group arrives at the bullring, Cohn elects to sit up high with Brett and Mike. Confident that he will be able to withstand the brutality of the fights, Cohn in fact says that he is afraid he might be "bored." This enrages Bill, who returns with Jake to the hotel for field glasses and wineskins. There they see Montoya, who asks them if they would like to meet Pedro Romero. In a hotel room surrounded by his handlers, Romero seems both inexperienced and heroic: "He was standing, straight and handsome and altogether by himself, alone in the room with the hangers-on." Jake and Bill return to the bullfight, where they occasionally turn their field glasses on Brett, Mike, and Cohn—who admits, when the fight ends, that he did feel a bit sickened by the slaughter of the horses.

Jake reports on the second day of bullfighting more fully than the first, comparing the "purity of line" in Romero's movements with the showy tricks of the other bullfighters. After the second fight, Mike says, only partially in jest, that he is afraid Brett is "falling in love with this bull-fighter chap." As the chapter ends, Jake notes that Romero does not go into the ring for two more days. "But all day and all night the fiesta kept on."

The conflicts leading to the novel's climax intensify in **chapter sixteen**, which begins with a description of how the fiesta goes on despite dreary weather. Early in the chapter, Jake advises Montoya not to give Romero an invitation from the American ambassador, as neither man wants to see the brilliant Romero flattered and corrupted. But at dinner, Romero's table is next to Jake's friends, who are engaging in drunken antics. As Jake attempts to have a serious conversation with Romero about his work, Mike repeatedly shouts, "Tell him that bulls have no balls!" Romero is drinking cognac with Jake and his friends when Montoya enters the room—and Montoya makes no pretense that his friendship with Jake will endure this betrayal. Romero soon leaves and Mike begins to attack Cohn, shouting at him to "take that sad Jewish face away." When Cohn refuses, the two prepare to fight, but Jake, acting as a "steer" among two bulls, stops them by taking Mike away.

After noting a number of English tourists at the crowded café tables, Bill and Mike take up with a girl named Edna and go "fiesta the English," as Bill expresses it, while Brett, Jake, and Cohn sit at a table in a rough pub called the Bar Milano. At this point, Brett loses patience with Cohn, sends him away (although he lingers outside), and then confesses to Jake that she is madly in love with Romero. When Jake advises her to try to stop feeling that way, she says, "How can I stop it? I can't stop things." Brett says that she must do this—consummate this feeling—to regain her self-respect after her affair with Cohn, although she also admits, "I do feel such a bitch." Jake takes Brett to Romero's table in the café and leaves her with him.

Events come to a climax in **chapter seventeen**, when we see why Cohn was once middleweight boxing champion of Princeton. After leaving Brett with Romero, Jake returns to Bill and Mike, who have been picking fights with the English tourists despite Edna's attempts to keep them out of trouble. Just as the four sit down to coffee at the Café Suizo, Cohn comes up and demands to know where Brett is. When Bill shouts that Brett is with the bullfighter, Cohn calls Jake a "pimp" and Jake takes a swing at him. Cohn then knocks Jake out cold and Bill to the floor.

As Jake recovers his senses, he says that "it all seemed like some bad play." But on the way back to the hotel, he finds that the world looks new and changed, as when he was once kicked in the head during a football game. When he gets to the hotel, he longs for a bath, but is met by Bill, who tells him to go upstairs and see Cohn. Jake goes to Cohn's room reluctantly and finds him lying on the bed, crying. Jake notes that he is wearing the sort of polo shirt he wore at Princeton, the place that saw him become a boxing champion but that nevertheless treated him as an outsider. Cohn tells Jake that he acted as he did because he was so in love with Brett. He tells Jake that he is leaving in the morning and begs him to shake hands, which Jake does, although to him it is a meaningless gesture.

The next morning Jake, following Bill, Mike, and Edna to the ring, sees a man gored on the way to the bullfight—fatally, it turns out. After describing the man's funeral, Jake tells us that the bull who had gored him was killed later that day by Romero, its ear cut off and given by Romero to Brett, who left it, wrapped in one of Jake's handkerchiefs, in a drawer in the hotel.

Later that day, Jake learns from Bill and Mike that, after knocking him down, Cohn broke in on Brett and Romero and "massacred the poor, bloody bull-fighter." Romero refused to give up even though he was clearly outmatched: When Cohn said he was too ashamed to hit Romero again, the young man continued to attack him with all his strength, exhibiting Hemingway's much-vaunted "grace under pressure" as he bravely battled an opponent he could not hope to overcome. Unlike Jake, Romero refused to shake hands, and Cohn left the scene a "ruined" man.

As **chapter eighteen** opens, we see that even on its final day, the force of the fiesta is strong enough to absorb "even the Biarritz English so that you did not see them unless you passed close to a table." Brett approaches Bill, Jake, and Mike sitting in the café, asks if Cohn is gone, and tells them how much he had hurt Romero the night before. At this point, Mike taunts Brett about her "Jew" and her "boy friend" and overturns the café table in a rage. Brett leaves the café with Jake. They go into the cathedral of San Fermin, as Brett says she would like to pray for Romero, but soon she asks to leave because the church makes her "damned nervous." Yet as they return to the hotel, Jake notes that Brett is happier and more carefree now that Cohn is gone.

At the hotel, Brett goes into Romero's room; Jake puts a drunken Mike to bed. He and Bill leave the hotel for lunch and then go to the café where they watch the fiesta "come to the boiling-point." When Brett appears, all three go with the crowd to the bullring to watch a bruised and swollen Romero perform. During the fights, Brett holds Romero's cape, which is stiff with blood. Jake describes the bullfights in great detail, comparing Romero to the other matadors. He notices that during the second of Romero's matches, his swollen face becomes less noticeable: "The fight with Cohn had not touched his spirit but his face had been smashed and his body hurt. He was wiping all that out now." After his second kill, Romero gives the bull's ear to Brett; she hands him his cape before he is lifted by the crowd and carried from the ring.

That afternoon Jake becomes very depressed as he sits in the café with Bill. He is drunk when he returns to the hotel and learns from Mike that Brett and Romero have left Pamplona on the seven o'clock train. Later, at dinner with Bill and Mike, Jake feels "as though about six people were missing."

In **book three**, the festival of San Fermin comes to an end (**chapter nineteen**). Jake, Mike, and Bill decide to leave Pamplona and drive to Bayonne, then to Biarritz, and leave Mike, who is broke, at Saint Jean de Luz, where he claims he can "live on tick" at a pub. After Jake sees Bill off from the Bayonne train station, he—alone now—goes to the hotel and is given the same room he had stayed in when he, Bill, and Cohn met in Bayonne on the way to Spain. Jake eats dinner in the hotel and explains his theory of tipping waiters well in France, where no one "makes things complicated by becoming your friend for any obscure reason."

The next day he heads back into Spain to take a holiday in San Sebastian—where Brett has recently been with both Cohn and Mike. He reads, bathes in the sea, and spends an evening with a group of French bicycle racers. But soon he receives two identical telegrams, one forwarded from Paris, the other from Pamplona: "COULD YOU COME HOTEL MONTANA MADRID AM RATHER IN TROUBLE BRETT." Jake immediately wires Brett that he will be arriving in Madrid the next day, and then muses to himself, "That was it. Send a girl off with one man. Introduce her to another to go off with him. Now go and bring her back. And sign the wire with love." Yet by going to "rescue" her in Madrid, he is exhibiting his own brand of grace under pressure—less showy than Romero's, but still authentic.

At the Hotel Montana in Madrid, Jake finds Brett alone and distraught but gratified that she, like Romero himself through his bullfight, has "wiped out that damned Cohn." But now she has sent Romero away because she does not want to ruin him. Although she is incapable of doing any good, she finds that she can make a personal sacrifice to keep herself from doing evil.

"I'm not going to be one of those bitches that ruins children," she tells Jake, although she cries in his arms after saying it. Later, though, in a bar she tells Jake that deciding "not to be a bitch" is "sort of what we have instead of God"—as Jake, earlier, had stumbled toward a vision of morality as the avoidance of self-disgust.

They have lunch, and Jake eats and drinks so heavily that Brett grows slightly alarmed and remarks on how much he likes consuming. But, as he puts it with barely repressed pain, "I like to do a lot of things"—referring, presumably, to the chief thing he would like to do but must finally resign himself to never being able to do. As they sit next to each other in a taxi after lunch—reminding the reader of Jake's earlier scenes with the prostitute and then with Brett herself—Brett tells Jake, "We could have had such a damned good time together." "Yes," Jake responds, "isn't it pretty to think so?" ❖

—*Anne Horn*
Bryn Mawr College

List of Characters

Jake Barnes is an American expatriate living in Paris. Emasculated in a World War I injury, he is unable to have a sexual relationship with the woman he loves, Brett Ashley. Although Jake works as a journalist for the *Herald Tribune,* he spends most of his time in Parisian bars and cafés, numbing his pain through liquor and superficial friendships. Unable to experience sexual passion, Jake has an *aficion*—passion based on knowledge—for bullfighters and bullfighting. He lives for the two weeks each year he spends at the festival of San Fermin in Madrid. Jake often functions in the novel like the steers who attempt to calm the bulls as they are unloaded before a bullfight: He is the peacemaker among a group of angry and bitter friends. But as the novel progresses, Jake's stoic acceptance of what life has to offer him reveals true heroic qualities: courage and grace.

Robert Cohn is also an expatriate American living in Paris. He has written a successful novel and is described as handsome, rich, and athletic. He is also Jewish, which makes him the target of many anti-Semitic attacks from the novel's characters. He is, nonetheless, an immature and aggravating figure. Although he has been given many advantages, he allows himself to be insulted and preyed upon. He falls childishly in love with the worldly Brett Ashley and follows her to Spain, even though she is traveling with her fiancé, Mike Campbell. Throughout the novel, Cohn is consistently out of sync with the other characters: He is sober when they are drunk, anticipates boredom when they are excited, falls asleep during the most intense moments of the fiesta. Although—as former middleweight champion—he easily knocks down the virile bullfighter Pedro Romero, Cohn is anything but heroic. By the end of the novel, when Jake's quiet heroism becomes most apparent, Cohn—who dominates the earlier chapters—has been banished from the book.

Brett Ashley is an Englishwoman who has an aristocratic title as a result of her marriage to a brutal lord. She loves Jake, who loves her in return although he knows that she marries for money, drinks too much, and indulges in meaningless sexual encounters. Brett makes repeated references to needing to bathe herself and is unwelcome or "damned nervous" in church. Despite her high social position, she is unclean—a destructive, vampire-like figure who uses men and then discards them. But after seducing the brilliant young bullfighter Pedro Romero, Brett decides to let him go because she does not want to destroy him. Although she is unable to do positive good, she can at least decide not to do evil. This, she tells Jake, is what she has "instead of God."

Pedro Romero is a nineteen-year-old bullfighter who seems to be the embodiment of Hemingway's heroic ideal. He is honorable, virile, and courageous, showing "grace under pressure" in the bullring. We see his heroism when he is faced with blows by boxing champion Robert Cohn. Although Romero is grossly outmatched, he refuses to give up the fight, so that Cohn must retreat in self-disgust. It is Romero's purity likewise that causes Brett to give him up. Although an inexperienced youth, he appears to be immune to corruption.

Bill Gorton is an American writer who has come to Europe to take a holiday with Jake. The novel's dialogue reveals him to be an amusing and witty man who also has a mean and racist side. Significantly, he is the only male character of any importance who does not fall in love with Brett. This spares him the suffering endured by Jake, Mike, and Cohn, but also prevents him from exhibiting Jake's admirable stoicism. Less pathetic and bitter than Cohn or Mike, Bill is also less heroic than Jake.

Mike Campbell is Brett's fiancé. Although he is bankrupt, he is likely to inherit money from his wealthy family. An upper-class Scot, he is also a nasty and bitter drunkard who shows very little capacity to accept Brett's behavior. By the end of the novel, he is almost as pathetic as the man he loathes—Cohn. Yet unlike Cohn, Mike does not become an outcast. Although chastened, he remains a member of Jake's social group. ❖

Critical Views

F. Scott Fitzgerald on Flaws in *The Sun Also Rises*

[F. Scott Fitzgerald (1896–1940), author of *The Great Gatsby* (1925) and a leading novelist of the "Lost Generation," was a close friend of Hemingway's. In this extract, Fitzgerald gives his evaluation of *The Sun Also Rises* after reading the novel in manuscript, remarking that some points are verbose and other parts snobbish.]

Anyhow I think parts of *Sun Also* are careless + ineffectual. As I said yesterday (and, as I recollect, in trying to get you to cut the 1st part of 50 Grand) I find in you the same tendency to envelope or (and as it usually turns out) to *embalm* in mere wordiness an anecdote or joke that casually appealed to you, that I find in myself in trying to preserve a piece of "fine writing." Your first chapter contains about 10 such things and it gives a feeling of condescending *casuallness*. ⟨. . .⟩

Pps. 1 + 2. Snobbish (not in itself but because the history of English Aristocrats in the war, set down so verbosely so uncritically, so exteriorly and yet so obviously inspired from within, is *shopworn*.) You had the same problem that I had with my Rich Boy, previously debauched by Chambers ect. Either bring more thot to it with the realization that that ground has already raised its wheat + weeds or cut it down to seven sentences. It hasn't even your rhythm and the fact that may be "true" is utterly immaterial.
—F. Scott Fitzgerald, Letter to Ernest Hemingway (June 1926), *Antaeus* No. 33 (Spring 1979): 15–16

Ernest Hemingway on the Purpose of *The Sun Also Rises*

[Hemingway paid careful attention to the opinions of fellow writers and reviewers of his work. In this extract, he takes note of a review of *The Sun Also Rises* and goes on to explain his own views on the purpose of his novel and the manner of its writing and revision.]

The point of the book to me was that the earth abideth forever—having a great deal of fondness and admiration for the earth and not a hell of a lot for my generation and caring little about Vanities. I only hesitated at the start to cut the writing of a better writer—but it seems necessary. I didn't mean the book to be a hollow or bitter satire but a damn tragedy with the earth abiding for ever as the hero.

Also have discovered that most people don't think in words—as they do in everybody's writing now—and so in Sun A.R. the critics miss their interior monologues and aren't happy—or disappointed I cut out 40,000 words of the stuff that would have made them happy out of the first Mss—it would have made them happy but it would have rung as false 10 years from now as Bromfield.

The Sun Also rises could have been and should have been a better book—but first Don Stewart was taking a cure for his liver in Vichy while I wrote the first draft of S.A.R. instead—and secondly I figure it is better to write about what you can write about and try and make it come off than have epoch making canvasses etc.—and you figure what age the novelists had that wrote the really great novels.

There can be the tour de force by a kid like [Stephen Crane in] *The Red Badge of Courage*—but in general they were pretty well along and they knew a few things—and in the time they were learning and going through it they learned how to write by writing.
    —Ernest Hemingway, Letter to Maxwell Perkins (19 November 1926), *Selected Letters,* ed. Carlos Baker (New York: Scribner's, 1981), pp. 229–30

ALLEN TATE ON *THE SUN ALSO RISES* AND *IN OUR TIME*

[Allen Tate (1899–1979) was a celebrated American poet and critic whose critical writings include *Essays on*

Poetry and Ideas (1936), *On the Limits of Poetry* (1948), and *Essays of Four Decades* (1969). In this review of *The Sun Also Rises,* Tate compares the novel with its predecessor, *In Our Time.*]

The present novel by the author of *In Our Time* supports the recent prophecy that he will be the "big man in American letters." At the time the prophecy was delivered it was meaningless because it was equivocal. Many of the possible interpretations now being eliminated, we fear it has turned out to mean something which we shall regret. Mr. Hemingway has written a book that will be talked about, praised, perhaps imitated; it has already been received in something of that cautiously critical spirit which the followers of Henry James so notoriously maintain toward the master. Mr. Hemingway has produced a successful novel, but not without returning some violence upon the integrity achieved in his first book. He decided for reasons of his own to write a popular novel, or he wrote the only novel which he could write.

To choose the latter conjecture is to clear his intentions, obviously at the cost of impugning his art. One infers moreover that although sentimentality appears explicitly for the first time in his prose, it must have always been there. Its history can be constructed. The method used in *In Our Time* was *pointilliste,* and the sentimentality was submerged. With great skill he reversed the usual and most general formula of prose fiction: instead of selecting the details of physical background and of human behavior for the intensification of a dramatic situation, he employed the minimum of drama for the greatest possible intensification of the observed object. The reference of emphasis for the observed object was therefore not the action; rather, the reference of the action was the object, and the action could be impure or incomplete without risk of detection. It could be mixed and incoherent; it could be brought in when it was advantageous to observation, or left out. The exception, important as such, in Mr. Hemingway's work is the story of Mr. and Mrs. Elliott. Here the definite dramatic conflict inherent in a sexual relation emerged as fantasy, and significantly; presumably he could not handle it otherwise without giving himself away.

In *The Sun Also Rises*, a full-length novel, Mr. Hemingway could not escape such leading situations, and he had besides to approach them with a kind of seriousness. He fails. It is not that Mr. Hemingway is, in the term which he uses in the contempt for the big word, hard-boiled; it is that he is not hard-boiled enough, in the artistic sense. No one can dispute with a writer the significance he derives from his subject-matter; one can only point out that the significance is mixed or incomplete. Brett is a nymphomaniac; Robert Cohn, a most offensive cad; both are puppets. For the emphasis is false; Hemingway doesn't fill out his characters and let them stand for themselves; he isolates one or two chief traits which reduce them to caricature. His perception of the physical object is direct and accurate; his vision of character, singularly oblique. And he actually betrays the interior machinery of his hard-boiled attitude: "It is awfully easy to be hard-boiled about everything in the daytime, but at night it is another thing," says Jake, the sexually impotent, musing on the futile accessibility of Brett. The history of his sentimentality is thus complete.

—Allen Tate, "Hard-Boiled," *Nation*, 15 December 1926, pp. 642–44

❖

EDMUND WILSON ON HEMINGWAY'S MORALITY IN *THE SUN ALSO RISES*

[Edmund Wilson (1895–1972) was perhaps the foremost American literary critic of the first half of the twentieth century. Among his many critical studies are *Axel's Castle* (1931) and *Patriotic Gore: Studies in the Literature of the American Civil War* (1962). In this extract, Wilson attempts to place *The Sun Also Rises* within the developing body of Hemingway's work, noting also its complex moral bearing.]

The barbarity of the world since the War is also the theme of Hemingway's next book, *The Sun Also Rises*. By his title and by the quotations which he prefixes to this book, he makes it plain what moral judgment we are to pass on the events he describes: "You are all a lost generation." What gives the book its profound unity and its disquieting effectiveness is the intimate relation established between the Spanish fiesta with its processions, its revelry and its bull-fighting and the atrocious behavior of the group of Americans and English who have come down from Paris to enjoy it. In the heartlessness of these people in their treatment of one another, do we not find the same principle at work as in the pagan orgy of the festival? Is not the brutal persecution of the Jew as much a natural casualty of a barbarous world as the fate of the man who is accidentally gored by the bull on the way to the bull-ring? The whole interest of *The Sun Also Rises* lies in the attempts of the hero and the heroine to disengage themselves from this world, or rather to arrive at some method of living in it honorably. The real story is the story of their attempts to do this—attempts by which, in such a world, they are always bound to lose in everything except honor. I do not agree, as has sometimes been said, that the behavior of the people in *The Sun Also Rises* is typical of only a small and special class of American and English expatriates. I believe that it is more or less typical of certain phases of the whole western world today; and the title *In Our Time* would have applied to it with as much appropriateness as to its predecessor.

Hemingway's attitude, however, toward the cruelties and treacheries he describes is quite different from anything else which one remembers in a similar connection. He has nothing of the generous indignation of the romantics: he does not, like Byron, bid the stones of the prisoner's cell "appeal from tyranny to God"; nor, like Shelley, bid the winds to "wail for the world's wrong." Nor has he even that grim and repressed, but still generous, still passionate feeling which we find in the pessimist-realists—in Hardy's *Tess,* in Maupassant's *Boule de Suif,* even in those infrequent scenes of Flaubert where we are made to boil at the spectacle of an old farm servant or of a young silk-weaver's daughter at the mercy of the bourgeoisie. In his treatment of the War, for example, Hemingway is as far as possible from Barbusse or from John Dos Passos. His point of view, his state of mind, is a curious one, and one typical of the time—he seems so broken in to the agonies of humanity, and, though even against his will, so impassively resigned to them, that his only protest is, as it were, the grin and the oath of the sportsman who loses the game. Furthermore, we are not always quite sure on which side Hemingway is betting. We are sometimes afflicted by the suspicion that what we are witnessing is a set-up, with the manager backing the barbarian. Yet, to speak of Hemingway in these terms is really to misrepresent him. He is not a moralist staging a melodrama, but an artist presenting a situation of which the moral values are complex. Hemingway thoroughly enjoys bull-fighting, as he enjoys skiing, racing, and prize-fights; and he is unremittingly conscious of the fact that, from the point of view of life as a sport, all that seems to him most painful is somehow closely bound up with what seems to him most enjoyable. The peculiar conflicts of feeling which arise in a temperament of this kind, are the subject of his fiction. His most remarkable effects, effects unlike anything else one remembers, are those, as in the fishing trip in *The Sun Also Rises,* where we are made to feel, behind the appetite for the physical world, the falsity or the tragedy of a moral situation. The inescapable consciousness of this discord does not arouse Hemingway to passionate violence; but it poisons him and makes him sick, and thus invests with a singular sinister quality—a quality perhaps new in fiction—the sunlight and the green summer landscapes of *The Sun Also Rises.* Thus, if Hemingway is oppressive, as Mr. Dodd complains, it is because he himself is oppressed. And we may find in him—in the clairvoyant's crystal of that incomparable art—an image of the common oppression.

—Edmund Wilson, "The Sportsman's Tragedy," *New Republic,* 14 December 1927, pp. 102–3

VIRGINIA WOOLF ON HEMINGWAY'S UNREALISTIC CHARACTERS

[Virginia Woolf (1882–1941), a celebrated British novelist, was also a penetrating essayist and reviewer.

Among her critical works are *The Common Reader* (1925) and *A Room of One's Own* (1929), a landmark work of feminist criticism. In this extract, Woolf believes that Hemingway's characters are neither as rich as those in other fictional works nor true to life.]

Recalling *The Sun Also Rises,* certain scenes rise in memory: the bullfight, the character of the Englishman, Harris; here a little landscape which seems to grow behind the people naturally; here a long, lean phrase which goes curling round a situation like the lash of a whip. Now and again this phrase evokes a character brilliantly, more often a scene. Of character, there is little that remains firmly and solidly elucidated. Something indeed seems wrong with the people. If we place them (the comparison is bad) against Tchekov's people, they are flat as cardboard. If we place them (the comparison is better) against Maupassant's people they are crude as a photograph. If we place them (the comparison may be illegitimate) against real people, the people we liken them to are of an unreal type. They are people one may have seen showing off at some café; talking a rapid, high-pitched slang, because slang is the speech of the herd, seemingly much at their ease, and yet if we look at them a little from the shadow not at their ease at all, and, indeed, terribly afraid of being themselves, or they would say things simply in their natural voices. So it would seem that the thing that is faked is character; Mr. Hemingway leans against the flanks of that particular bull after the horns have passed.

—Virginia Woolf, "An Essay in Criticism" (1927), *Collected Essays,* ed. Leonard Woolf (New York: Harcourt, Brace & World, 1967), Vol. 2, p. 255

MARK SCHORER ON THE SYMBOLISM OF BULLFIGHTING

[Mark Schorer (1908–1977), who taught at Harvard University and the University of California at Berkeley, was a prolific novelist, short story writer, critic, and biographer. He wrote *William Blake: The Politics of*

Vision (1946), *Modern British Fiction* (1961), and *Sinclair Lewis: An American Life* (1961). In this extract, Schorer probes the symbolism of bullfighting in *The Sun Also Rises,* remarking as well on some features of Hemingway's prose.]

The Sun Also Rises was a representation of the life that Hemingway lived and enjoyed and out of which his values came. The characters in this novel—without belief, without relation to a cultural or national past, without ideological relation to the future—submerge themselves in extravagant sensation and view life as a losing game, a sport like bullfighting which, while it is more nearly tragedy than sport because death is inevitable, is interesting only if it observes strict rules. Hemingway epitomized this not very difficult matter when, in an author's note in *Scribner's Magazine,* he once said, "I've known some very wonderful people who even though they were going directly to the grave . . . managed to put up a very fine performance enroute." This "fine performance" is the sporting attitude, and it is dramatized in the gesture of Lady Ashley when she gives up her lover: "You know I feel rather damned good, Jake . . . it makes one feel rather good deciding not to be a bitch. . . . It's sort of what we have instead of God." Jake has himself observed that morality is what makes you feel good afterwards. Brett feels "rather damned good" because she has behaved according to the tenets of that negative morality, that emphasis on the "performance en route," the *manner* of living, which the group has substituted for belief.

The preoccupation with bullfighting is not accidental; bullfighting is at once the most violent and the most stylized of sports. Its entire excitement depends on the degree to which the matador exposes himself to death *within the rules.* It disregards consequences, regards performance. Both are important. Courage, or unconcern for disaster, is a moral virtue: the best bullfighter works closest to the horns; the best man disregards present and impending catastrophe. Syphilis, the occupational disease of bullfighters, "of all people who lead lives in which a disregard of consequences dominate," is nearly commended. A blundering display of courage, however, is absurd: the matador should "increase the amount of the danger of death" *within the rules provided for his protection.* . . . it is to his credit if he does something that he knows how to do in a highly dangerous but still geometrically possible manner. It is to his discredit if he runs danger through ignorance, through disregard of the fundamental rules. . . .

Courage stylized, *style,* then, matters finally, and the experienced spectator looks for this: "what they seek is honesty and true, not tricked, emotion and always classicism and the purity of execution of all the suertes, and . . . they want no sweetening." Since the performance is a matter of the fighter's honor, bullfighting is a *moral* art, and style a *moral* matter.

So far, about morals, [writes Hemingway] I know only what is moral is what you feel good after and what is immoral is what you feel bad after and judged by these moral standards . . . the bullfight is very moral to me. . . .

In *The Sun Also Rises,* Romero, who "fakes" nothing in the fight, who has "the old thing, the holding of his purity of line through the maximum of exposure," is the one character who makes the others feel fine: he is the representation of artistic, hence of moral excellence.

All this carried directly over into Hemingway's concept of prose and into his own prose. The definition of morality and Brett's dramatization of it; the important counterpoint between danger and performance; the concept of art as moral insofar as its style is "honest" or "true" or "pure"—this complex is translated as follows:

It is much more difficult than poetry. . . . It can be written, *without tricks* and *without cheating. With nothing that will go bad afterwards.* . . . First, there must be talent. . . . Then there must be discipline. . . . Then there must be . . . an *absolute conscience* as unchanging as the standard meter in Paris, to prevent *faking.*

The style which made Hemingway famous—with its ascetic suppression of ornament and figure, its insistence on the objective and the unreflective (for good fighters do not talk), its habit of understatement (or sportsmen boast), the directions and the brevity of its syntactical constructions, its muscularity, the sharpness of its staccato and repetitive effects, "the purity of its line under the maximum of exposure," that is, its continued poise under the weight of event or feeling—this style is an exact transfiguration of Hemingway's moral attitude toward a peculiarly violent and chaotic experience. His style, in effect, is what he had instead of God.

Until God came.

—Mark Schorer, "The Background of a Style," *Kenyon Review* 3, No. 1 (Winter 1941): 101–3

❖

CARLOS BAKER ON BRETT ASHLEY AS A CIRCE FIGURE

[Carlos Baker (1909–1987) was the Woodrow Wilson Professor of Literature at Princeton University. He is the author of *Ernest Hemingway: A Life Story* (1969) and the editor of Hemingway's *Selected Letters* (1981). In this extract from his celebrated biographical study *Hemingway: The Writer as Artist* (1952), Baker maintains that Brett Ashley is a Circe figure and that *The Sun Also Rises* develops into a conflict between paganism and Christianity.]

Hemingway's first novel provides an important insight into the special "mythological" methods which he was to employ with increasing assurance and success in the rest of his major writing. It is necessary to distinguish Hemingway's method from such "mythologizing" as that of Joyce in *Ulysses*, or Eliot in *The Waste Land*. For Hemingway early devised and subsequently developed a mythologizing tendency of his own which does not depend on antecedent literatures, learned footnotes, or the recognition of spot passages. *The Sun Also Rises* is a first case in point.

It might be jocularly argued, for example, that there is much more to the portrait of Lady Brett Ashley than meets the non-Homeric eye. It is very pleasant to think of the Pallas Athene, sitting among the statuary in one of her temples like Gertrude Stein among the Picassos in the rue de Fleurus, and murmuring to the Achaeans, homeward bound from the battle of Troy: "You are all a lost generation." As for Brett, Robert Cohn calls her Circe. "He claims she turns men into swine," says Mike Campbell. "Damn good. I wish I were one of those literary chaps." If Hemingway had been writing about brilliant literary chaps in the manner, say, of Aldous Huxley in *Chrome Yellow,* he might have undertaken to develop Cohn's parallel. It would not have been farther-fetched than Joyce's use of the Daedalus legend in *A Portrait of the Artist* or Eliot's kidnapping of Homeric Tiresias to watch over the mean little seductions of *The Waste Land.*

Was not Brett Ashley, on her low-lying island in the Seine, just such a fascinating peril as Circe on Aeaea? Did she not open her doors to all the modern Achaean chaps? When they drank her special potion of French applejack or Spanish wine, did they not become as swine, or in the modern idiom, wolves? Did not Jake Barnes, that wily Odysseus, resist the shameful doom which befell certain of his less wary comrades who became snarling beasts?

There are even parallel passages. Says Jake Barnes, thinking of Brett: "I lay awake thinking and my mind jumping around. . . . Then all of a sudden I started to cry. Then after a while it was better . . . and then I went to sleep." Says Ulysses on Aeaea: "My spirit was broken within me and I wept as I sat on the bed. . . . But when I had my fill of weeping and writhing, I made answer." Or what shall be made of Robert Cohn, quietly and classically asleep on the winecasks in the back room of a Pamplona tavern, wreathed with twisted garlics and dead to the world while Brett and the others carouse in the room beyond? "There was one named Elpenor," says the *Odyssey,* "the youngest of all; not very valiant in war nor sound of understanding, who had laid him down apart from his comrades in the sacred house of Circe, seeking the cool air, for he was heavy with wine. He heard the noise and bustle of his comrades as they moved about."

If he had wished to follow the mythological method of Eliot's *Waste Land* or Joyce's *Ulysses,* Hemingway could obviously have done so. But his own esthetic opinions carried him away from the literary kind of myth-adaptation and over into that deeper area of psychological symbol-building which does not require special literary equipment to be interpreted. One needs only sympathy and a few degrees of heightened emotional awareness. The special virtue of this approach to the problem of literary communication is that it can be grasped by all men and women because they are human beings. None of the best writers are without it. It might even be described as the residuum of "natural knowledge" and belief, visible in every artist after the traditional elements have been siphoned off. This is perhaps roughly what Keats meant by saying that Shakespeare led a life of allegory, his works being the comments on it. Thoreau's phrase for the same thing, as R. L. Cook has pointed out, is "dusky knowledge." Pilar, the Cumaean sybil of *For Whom the Bell Tolls,* moves regularly in this half-subliminal area. She inherits her skill and discernment from Hemingway.

Under the matter-of-factness of the account of the feria of San Fermin a sabidurían symbolism is at work. It does not become formally apparent until the party has assembled to prepare for the festival. Then, in several ways, it develops as a dialectical struggle between paganism and Christian orthodoxy—a natural and brilliant use of the fact that the fiesta is both secular and religious, and that the *riau-riau* dancers unabashedly follow the procession which bears the patron saint through the streets of Pamplona.

The contrast is admirably dramatized through Jake and Brett. Without apology or explanation, Jake Barnes is a religious man. As a professing Catholic, he attends masses at the cathedral before and during fiesta week. On the Saturday before the festival opens, Brett accompanies him. "She said she wanted to hear me go to confession," says Jake, "but I told her that not only was it impossible but it was not as interesting as it sounded, and, besides, it would be in a language she did not know." Jake's remark can be taken doubly. The language Brett does not know is Latin; it is also Spanish; but it is especially the language of the Christian religion. When she goes soon afterwards to have her fortune told at a gypsy camp, Brett presumably hears language that she *can* understand.

—Carlos Baker, *Hemingway: The Writer as Artist* (Princeton: Princeton University Press, 1952), pp. 87–89

❖

DELMORE SCHWARTZ ON PLAYING BY THE RULES

[Delmore Schwartz (1913–1966), a noted American poet, fiction writer, and critic, was a longtime editor of the *Partisan Review*. His *Selected Essays* appeared in 1970, and *Portrait of Delmore: Journals and Notes 1939–1959* was published in 1986. In this extract, Schwartz asserts that a moral code of "playing by the rules" can be found in Hemingway's works and that Robert Cohn in *The Sun Also Rises* is a prominent violator of that code.]

The desire for sensation is not the sensuality of the dilettante, but a striving for genuine individuality. The sensations of the immediate present have an authenticity which the senses make self-evident. Above all, those sensations which occur in the face of grave physical danger reveal the self's essential reality, since in the face of extreme threat, the self must depend wholly upon its own skill, strength, and courage.

Thus it is literally true that Hemingway's preoccupation with sensation is a preoccupation with genuine selfhood, moral character, and conduct. The holiday provides not only freedom, but good eating, good drinking, good landscapes, and good sexual intercourse under conditions which have the fairness of a game—so that drinking, making love, and most of the pursuits of the holiday become a trial of the self. Any concern with the self and its moral character requires a moral code, and the moral code in Hemingway is unmistakable. The rules of the code require honesty, sincerity, self-control, skill, and above all, personal courage. To be admirable is to play fairly and well; and to be a good loser when one has lost, acknowledging the victor and accepting defeat in silence. It is a sportsmanlike morality, which dictates a particular kind of carriage, good manners, and manner of speech: one must speak in clipped tones, condensing the most complex emotion into a few expletives or into the dignity of silence.

Perhaps Cohn, in *The Sun Also Rises,* is the best example of the character who repeatedly violates the Hemingway code. He is rich, gifted, and skillful; he has gone to Princeton, where he excelled in boxing, and he is a novelist and editor. Yet these advantages are unavailing, for he does not play the game according to the rules. He discusses his emotions in great detail, refuses to admit defeat when Brett, the lady with whom he is in love, rejects him, and, when he is hurt, he insists on telling everyone, instead of suffering in silence. Thus he is one of the damned. His damnation shows itself most explicitly when he struggles with Romero, the matador who has won Lady Brett's heart. Unlike several other rejected suitors, Cohn refuses to admit defeat, or the lady's right to choose. Instead he engages the matador in a fist fight, knocks him down again and again, but cannot knock him out since the matador, a true Hemingway hero, takes interminable punishment, silently arising from the floor again and again until Cohn is finally defeated by the matador's fortitude and thus his moral superiority. In a like way, Lady Brett obeys the code and renounces the matador, when, coming to recognize that he fulfills an ideal of conduct as a human being and as a matador, she perceives that she is a threat to his purity: "It isn't the sort of thing one does," she says, adding that she does not want to be "one of these bitches who ruins children . . . it makes one feel rather good deciding not to be a bitch. . . . It's sort of what we have instead of God."

—Delmore Schwartz, "The Fiction of Ernest Hemingway," *Perspectives USA* (New York: Intercultural Publications, 1955), pp. 258–59

❖

MALCOLM COWLEY ON *THE SUN ALSO RISES* AS PRODUCT OF WORLD WAR I

[Malcolm Cowley (1898–1989) was an American poet and critic and close friend of Hemingway's. He is the author of many books, including *Exile's Return* (1934), *The Literary Situation* (1954), and *The Flower and the Leaf* (1985). In this extract from *A Second Flowering* (1956), Cowley studies *The Sun Also Rises* as a literary and moral product of World War I.]

The situation in the background of *The Sun Also Rises* is the Great War, in which most of the characters have served and in which some of them have been physically or morally wounded. All the characters except Pedro Romero, the matador, have lost their original code of values. Feeling the loss, they are now trying to live by a simpler code, essentially that of soldiers on furlough, and it is this effort that unites them as a group. "I told you he was one of us," Lady Brett says of Count Mippipopolous after he has unashamedly stripped off his shirt and shown them where an arrow had passed completely through his body. The unashamedness, the wound, and the courage it suggests are all things they have in common. The war has deadened some of their feelings and has left them capable of enjoying only the simplest and strongest pleasures. It has also given them an attitude of resigned acceptance toward all sorts of disasters, including those caused by their own follies. Robert Cohn, however, has never been wounded and has never learned to be resigned; therefore he refuses to let Brett go, fights with his rivals including Romero, and is cast out of the group. Romero is their simple-minded saint. Brett is almost on the point of permanently corrupting him, but she obeys another article of the code and draws back. "You know it makes one feel rather good deciding not to be a bitch," she says (and scores of junior Bretts have echoed). "It's sort of what we have instead of God."

The Sun Also Rises is not, as it is often called, Hemingway's best novel. After all it is his first, and there are signs in it of his struggle to master a new medium. In spite of his deletions from the manuscript, there are still details that do not seem essential, as notably in the street-by-street account of Jake Barnes's wanderings through Paris. There are also a few obvious guideposts for the reader, as when Jake says of Robert Cohn that "he was not so simple" after coming back from New York, "and he was not so nice." Although Cohn's fight with Romero is the physical climax of the action, it is reported at second hand—by Mike Campbell, who has heard the story from Brett, who was the only witness of the fight—instead of being directly presented. More serious than those technical flaws is the sort of timeliness that is always in danger of going stale. Brett was a pathetic brave figure for her time, but the pathos has been cheapened by thousands of imitation Bretts in life and fiction. Bill Gorton's remarks are not so bright now as they once seemed. "You're an expatriate," he tells Jake ironically. "You've lost touch with the soil. You get precious. Fake European standards have ruined you. . . . You hang around cafés." In those days, as I have been reminded by old newspaper clippings, editorial writers with nothing else to say used to deplore and deride the expatriates. Now that the editorials have been forgotten, a reader does not feel as he might have felt in 1926, that Gorton is making exactly the right rejoinder.

Not everything changes. After one has mentioned those wrinkles and scars revealed by age, how much of the novel seems as marvelously fresh as when it first appeared! Count Mippipopolous, his wound, and his champagne; the old couple from Montana on their first trip abroad; the busload of Basque peasants; the whole beautiful episode of the fishing trip in the mountains, in the harsh sunlight, with bright water tumbling over the dam; then by contrast the dark streets of Pamplona crowded with *riau-riau* dancers, who formed a circle round Brett as if she were a revered witch—as indeed she was, and as Jake in a way was the impotent Fisher King ruling over a sterile land—in all this there is nothing that has gone bad and not a word to be changed after so many years. It is all carved in stone, bigger and truer than life, and it is the work of a man who, having ended his busy term of apprenticeship, was already a master at twenty-six.

—Malcolm Cowley, "Hemingway in Paris," *A Second Flowering: Works and Days of the Lost Generation* (London: Andre Deutsch, 1956), pp. 71–73

❖

W. M. FROHOCK ON THE "LOST GENERATION"

[W. M. Frohock (1908–1984) taught at Brown, Wesleyan, and Harvard and wrote several critical works, including *Strangers to This Ground: Cultural Diversity in Contemporary American Writing* (1961) and *André Malraux and the Tragic Imagination* (1967).

In this extract from *The Novel of Violence in America* (1957), Frohock notes that by the 1950s it has become difficult to recapture the emotional atmosphere of the "Lost Generation" so keenly portrayed in *The Sun Also Rises.*]

In the light of the discipline, the emotional pattern of the book as a whole becomes important; and we had better reconstruct it, since the passing of time is obscuring it more and more, at least to the new reader. The whole job of reading this book has changed from what it was when it came out. The Lost Generation has achieved the dignity—and unreality—of a historical concept. It is increasingly hard to remember that the American expatriates of the middle twenties were serious artists and not spoiled brats; it may be too much to expect that a group which fled America because it did not feel emotionally secure and at home there should seem anything other than trivial to another generation which, after a different kind of war, is compellingly impressed by the insecurity of mere *physical* life anywhere on the planet.

Certainly Hemingway's despair, like that of Eliot in *The Waste Land,* is the kind which can be contemplated with leisure and some ease; it is despair without terror. As a matter of fact, the years of the great depression blunted its point; too many people discovered that it is even more important to eat regularly than to feel quite in place among one's contemporaries. And consequently it is easy to miss the essential datum, that the emotional mood of the first part of *The Sun Also Rises* is a ceaseless, dull ache. The reader is supposed to know that Jake's physical disability is in large part a symbol for the general feeling of frustration and pointlessness of life, that if Jake were physically qualified to possess Brett it would make very little difference, that Brett's nymphomania is really unimportant because if she ever managed to overcome it she would be accomplishing the eradication of a symptom without doing anything for the sickness of the soul. I should think that it might be impossible for anyone opening the book now to find anything much, other than irrelevant digression, in the pages about the self-made Greek Count whose fantastic wine-parties, of course, used to have so much to do with the reader's getting the mood of the whole first part—since Jake so palpably feels that while such things are not a very profitable occupation they are certainly as profitable as anything else.

Yet only if we understand the essential emotional mood of the first part of the book can we appreciate the careful balance between the emotions and the writing—otherwise there is no reasonable explanation for Hemingway's writing so completely under wraps. We risk seeing much more of the snaffle and the bit than we do of the bloody horse. Either we feel the appropriateness of the constant toning down of the whole Paris episode or it will seem like a somewhat staged preparation for the Spanish part, designed to make the latter look brilliant by contrast. We have to know that we get a scant and referential treatment of the Paris scene because Jake is so used to it, and it is so much a part of his dull ache that he does not really see it. We get some of the free-associative spoofing that Hemingway loves to do, about taxidermy and the possibility of stuffed dogs as gifts, but this, as compared with the lovely examples of the same stuff in the Burguete episode, is carefully restrained. The characters do not yet appear as particularly interesting people; we know that Cohn is an importunate romantic oaf, that Mike Campbell is a drunken chronic bankrupt, that Brett is a drunk with a tendency toward promiscuity—and even of her we get something short of a full picture until the Paris episode is over and we discover that she has been sleeping with Cohn, for whom she cares absolutely nothing. Of them all we know just enough so that nothing they do later in the story will catch us by surprise.

Hemingway's whole method in this first part is pretty well summed up in his description of Brett as she is riding with Jake in a taxi. It is night. Illumination is provided by an occasional shop window and by the flares of workmen who are repairing trolley tracks. All that you actually get of Brett (and here again Hemingway is sticking to his purpose of giving you what the character actually sees, not what he should see) is the whiteness of her face and the long line of her neck—even though these people are alone and they are as much in love as their personal disabilities will permit. Substitute in this instance the idea of emotion for light and you have Hemingway's guiding motive throughout the first part: he sees and says only what the abomination-of-desolation mood permits. Obviously, if the emotional climate should be lost on the reader, the whole point would also be lost.

—W. M. Frohock, "Ernest Hemingway: The River and the Hawk," *The Novel of Violence in America* (Dallas: Southern Methodist University Press, 1957), pp. 170–72

MARK SPILKA ON THE DEATH OF LOVE IN *THE SUN ALSO RISES*

[Mark Spilka (b. 1925) is a professor of English at Brown University and a leading literary scholar, who has written *The Love Ethic of D. H. Lawrence* (1955), *Virginia Woolf's Quarrel with Grieving* (1980), and *Hemingway's Quarrel with Androgyny* (1990). In this extract, Spilka argues that *The Sun Also Rises* uses the war and bullfighting as a means of conveying the death of love.]

One of the most persistent themes of the twenties was the death of love in World War I. All the major writers recorded it, often in piecemeal fashion, as part of the larger postwar scene; but only Hemingway seems to have caught it whole and delivered it in lasting fictional form. His intellectual grasp of the theme might account for this. Where D. H. Lawrence settles for the shock of the war on the Phallic Consciousness, or where Eliot presents assorted glimpses of sterility, Hemingway seems to design an extensive parable. Thus, in *The Sun Also Rises,* his protagonists are deliberately shaped as allegorical figures: Jake Barnes and Brett Ashley are two lovers desexed by the war; Robert Cohn is the false knight who challenges their despair; while Romero, the stalwart bullfighter, personifies the good life which will survive their failure. Of course, these characters are not abstractions in the text; they are realized through the most concrete style in American fiction, and their larger meaning is implied only by their response to immediate situations. But the implications are there, the parable is at work in every scene, and its presence lends unity and depth to the whole novel.

Barnes himself is a fine example of this technique. Cut off from love by a shell wound, he seems to suffer from an undeserved misfortune. But as most readers agree, his condition represents a peculiar form of emotional impotence. It does not involve distaste for the flesh, as with Lawrence's crippled veteran, Clifford Chatterley; instead Barnes lacks the power to control love's strength and durability. His sexual wound, the result of an unpreventable "accident" in the war, points to another realm where accidents can always happen and where Barnes is equally powerless to prevent them. In book 2 of the novel he makes this same comparison while describing one of the dinners at Pamplona: "It was like certain dinners I remember from the war. There was much wine, an ignored tension, and a feeling of things coming that you could not prevent happening." This fear of emotional consequences is the key to Barnes's condition. Like so many Hemingway heroes, he has no way to handle subjective complications, and his wound is a token for this kind of impotence.

It serves the same purpose for the expatriate crowd in Paris. In some figurative manner these artists, writers, and derelicts have all been rendered impotent by the war. Thus, as Barnes presents them, they pass before us like a parade of sexual cripples, and we are able to measure them against his own forbearance in the face of a common problem. Whoever bears his sickness well is akin to Barnes; whoever adopts false postures, or willfully hurts others, falls short of his example. This is the organizing principle in book 1, this alignment of characters by their stoic qualities. But stoic or not, they are all incapable of love, and in their sober moments they seem to know it.

—Mark Spilka, "The Death of Love in *The Sun Also Rises*," *Twelve Original Essays on Great American Novels*, ed. Charles Shapiro (Detroit: Wayne State University Press, 1958), pp. 238–40

❖

[Cleanth Brooks (b. 1906) is one of the leading American literary critics of our time. Among his many books are *Modern Poetry and the Tradition* (1939), *The Well Wrought Urn* (1947), and *William Faulkner: First Encounters* (1983). In this extract, Brooks finds that the values Hemingway asserts in *The Sun Also Rises* are compatible with Christianity.]

The virtues that Hemingway celebrates are narrower than those celebrated by political liberalism. They are much narrower than those affirmed by Christianity. There should be no illusion about this. But the virtues Hemingway celebrates are ultimately necessary to Christianity, and, as we have seen, they look toward Christianity. For they have everything to do with man's dignity as a free spirit—they're "spiritual" even though the irony is that the creature who yearns after them is in Hemingway's view a dying animal in a purely mechanistic universe.

It is almost as if Hemingway, driven back out of theism, dispossessed of his heritage, insists upon stubbornly defending whatever he has felt could still be held. It is a kind of rear-guard action that he fights. The point comes out clearly enough in his very first novel, *The Sun Also Rises*. As the book ends, Brett is talking to her friend Jake. Jake and Brett should be married to each other. They understand each other. There is a real bond between them. But fate has played one of its ugly tricks. Jake has been emasculated by a wound received in the war. No marriage between them is possible. Yet Brett relies upon Jake, and now, as the novel ends, she has wired him to come to Madrid to be with her. She has just left the young Spanish bullfighter to whom she has been tremendously attracted and whom she has proceeded to seduce. She has, however, almost immediately given him up because she has realized that she will ruin him and because she has told herself that "I'm not going to be one of those bitches that ruins children."

Brett confides to Jake something of the feelings that possess her at having made this gesture of denial. She tells Jake: "You know it makes one feel rather good deciding not to be a bitch," and when Jake says, "Yes," she goes on to say, "It's sort of what we have instead of God." Jake observes dryly that "Some people have God. Quite a lot." But neither he nor Brett has God, nor do most of the characters with whom Hemingway concerns himself. And perhaps this very honesty, this lack of sentimentality, this refusal to mix up categories, is the thing which makes Hemingway most useful to the reader who does have a religious commitment. Even men and women who do not have God must try to make up for him in some sense, quixotic as that gesture will seem and, in ultimate terms at least, desperate as that gesture must be. The Christian will feel that it is ultimately desperate in that man can never find anything that will prove a substitute for God. But the Christian will do well to recognize his God though hidden by the incognito which He sometimes assumes. Jake's courage is such an incognito and manifests the divine reality, though of course not fully and not in specifically religious terms.

Hemingway is perfectly right to confine himself to his secular terms. Artistic integrity, fidelity to his vision of reality, honesty in portraying the reactions of the Jakes and Bretts of our world—all conduce to this proper limitation. The Christian reader will therefore be very imperceptive if he fails to see how honestly and sensitively Hemingway has portrayed a situation that exists; he will show an unconscionable smugness if he fails to appreciate the gallantry of actions taken in full consciousness that there is no God to approve or sanction them. He will even hesitate to say "There but for the grace of God go I." For it might be presumptuous of him to assume that, deprived of grace, he could go at all along the road that Hemingway's heroes are forced to take.

—Cleanth Brooks, "Ernest Hemingway: Man on His Moral Uppers," *The Hidden God: Studies in Hemingway, Faulkner, Yeats, Eliot, and Warren* (New Haven: Yale University Press, 1963), pp. 20–21

❖

[Sheldon Norman Grebstein (b. 1928) is the president of the State University of New York at Purchase. He is the author of *Sinclair Lewis* (1962) and *John O'Hara* (1966) and the editor of *Perspectives in Contemporary Criticism* (1968). In this extract from *Hemingway's Craft* (1973), Grebstein discusses how dialogue is used to portray character in *The Sun Also Rises*.]

One of the valuable yet subtle techniques of characterization through dialogue in *The Sun Also Rises* is the contrast drawn between public and private conversations. This contrast signifies the large opposition between the "in" and "out" groups of characters and is thus integral to theme. From the start Jake makes it plain that among his objections to Cohn and Cohn's crowd, the expatriate poseurs, is Cohn's inability to keep private feelings out of public conversations. We notice this at once when Cohn confesses his fears about the transience of life and his desire to go to South America before it's too late, exposing a juvenile attitude he ought to have concealed. The indictment against Cohn becomes really severe, however, when Jake witnesses the nasty scene in which Frances Clyne airs her resentments and ridicules Cohn while he sits there and takes it. In contrast, Jake's hopeless love for Brett and the agony it entails are restricted to scenes known to themselves alone. Publicly Jake and Brett converse in laconic exchanges made up largely of terse witticisms and cryptic allusions. The same contrast prevails through the novel, with a few interesting and notable variations.

When the in-group characters drink, they are liable to say too much and violate the protocols of restraint. This is exactly the situation in chapter 13, when, parallel to Frances's earlier, sober humiliation of Cohn, Mike launches into him and vilifies him in front of the others, shaming himself as well as Cohn by betraying emotions more properly kept under guard. Even Brett, consummate actress that she is in maintaining her bluff English stoicism, tends to let herself go in drink and become too noisy and a little abusive. We observe this in chapter 7, when Brett's jibes against Count Mippopopolous, "Don't be an ass. . . . You haven't any values. You're dead, that's all," rebound off the Count's imperturbable dignity to Brett's own discredit. In drink she can also be careless with Jake's feelings, as at the end of chapter 4.

Hemingway portrays the contrast between the characters drunk and sober not only by the content of their remarks but by quantity and diction as well. When Brett is sober and alone with Jake she tends to speak in clear and standard diction, and in complete sentences. In public, or tipsy, she lapses into fragmentary bits of speech, dropping subjects, verbs, or pronouns, and/or into Brittish colloquialisms. Depending on the context, the effect is either mannered (public) or reckless (drunk). Mike is drunk from the beginning to almost the end, but before the Pamplona sequence he masquerades as feckless jester, asserting his presence with quips and witticisms. But in chapter 13 he steps front and center and delivers a barrage of remarks in consecutive volleys, punctuating his attack with the repeated reference to Cohn as a "bloody steer." Bill is another character who, sober, is normally terse and rather inconspicuous but ungrammatically magniloquent in drink, fixating on a word or phrase and worrying it endlessly.

—Sheldon Norman Grebstein, *Hemingway's Craft* (Carbondale: Southern Illinois University Press, 1973), pp. 116–17

W. J. STUCKEY ON ROMANTICISM IN *THE SUN ALSO RISES*

[W. J. Stuckey (b. 1923), former professor of English at Purdue University, has written a study of Caroline Gordon (1972) and *The Pulitzer Prize Novels: A Critical Backward Look* (1981). In this extract, Stuckey offers a general analysis of *The Sun Also Rises*, finding it to embody a kind of romanticism in its blend of self-indulgence and self-control.]

The Sun Also Rises, then, is largely a book about pleasure, masculine pleasure, a kind of puritan hedonist's manual. Enjoy but control. That is the book's surface message (if it can be said to have one) and the fact that it continues to interest and even excite readers is a testimony not perhaps to the soundness of Hemingway's philosophy but to the soundness of his art. He found exactly the right set of circumstances and the right set of characters to exemplify his theme, or perhaps—for this is an autobiographical book—he found in his own experiences and observations exactly what it was that made him feel that this was true, and he expressed it with restraint and economy as well as with pleasure. 'Enjoy' and 'control' are not very close in meaning to the words of Buddha that conclude *The Waste Land*. Give. Sympathize. Control. But they are close to Hemingway's habitual themes.

Those who respond to *The Sun Also Rises* with a different set of assumptions and a different way of feeling will doubtless find this reading inadequate for explaining what is clearly (at least from another point of view) a set of irresponsible characters going through meaningless actions, but this is not a judgment Hemingway would have made nor one that we are invited to make either. If we see *The Waste Land* in *The Sun Also Rises*, that is because we are prepared to find it there, and of course there is no reason why one cannot read Hemingway's novel symptomatically. He was writing about the world as he knew it, the same world that Eliot wrote about, and it may be that in treating his material objectively he inadvertently and unintentionally revealed the emotional hollowness that Eliot consciously and critically exposed. It may be the emotional emptiness, the absence of traditional manifestations of romantic love that make one feel—even if the waste land symbol is spurious—that Hemingway has indeed created his own version of *The Waste Land*.

The difference, of course, is more than a matter of consciousness. Eliot reacted with horror to what Hemingway treated with ironic detachment. Eliot's poem is an outcry against perversions of the spirit, Hemingway's novel is an extended definition of pleasure and a protest against the romantic "lies" that would spoil it by substituting for actual experience half-baked theories about it.

Of course, *The Sun Also Rises* has its own form of romanticism, a special blending of self-indulgence and self-control, a love for and a hatred of life because, though sweet, life must end. It comes out—this romanticism—in a need to confront life not only directly but with violent calm, offering oneself as the bull fighter does to a force that will eventually destroy him but which for a time he can control and master. It is in this confrontation that love and hate are balanced and the tension between them is released, in fishing, in bull fighting. In love, or in sex that is more than a brief relationship, tension grows, demands are made, obligations incurred, jealousies aroused. Life grows messy and complicated. One cannot any longer do the simple things that give so much pleasure.

In a letter to Archibald MacLeish, Hemingway said that *The Sun Also Rises* was a book about promiscuity; however, it is not the illicit aspect of the various relationships with Brett that is destructive, but the sexual relationship itself; and the more permanent it becomes (as with Romero), the more deadly. One thinks of Nick and George skiing in "Cross-Country Snow" and lamenting that their skiing days are over. Nick is married and about to become a father and return home and settle down. "Maybe we'll never go skiing again, Nick," George says. Nick replies, "We've got to. It isn't worthwhile if you can't." Growing up, getting married, family responsibility—all get in the way of things that matter most to Hemingway. And Brett, being the right sort, recognizes the inevitable and calls off her affair with Romero before it becomes permanently destructive. But Brett is still something of a romantic herself. After all she has been through, she still believes that she and Jake could have "had such a good time together."

The title of this novel and the biblical verses from which it comes catch very nicely the romantic attitude that underlies *The Sun Also Rises,* that disputes Brett's words and pervades not only this work but so much of Hemingway's fiction—an attitude that says, with chin up and lowered eyes, that we are all bitched from the start but that we must live with the knowledge of death and extinction, taking what pleasure we can from the sensuous contemplation of that fact and some little

comfort in the permanence of nature itself; generations pass away, but the earth abides. The belief that man can ever be happy for long in any human relationship, even in joyous Spain, is to be smiled at a little sadly. "Isn't it pretty to think so?"
—W. J. Stuckey, *"The Sun Also Rises* on Its Own Ground," *Journal of Narrative Technique* 6, No. 3 (Fall 1976): 229–30

❖

JOYCE CAROL OATES ON *THE SUN ALSO RISES* AND *THE GREAT GATSBY*

[Joyce Carol Oates (b. 1938) is one of the most important contemporary novelists; among her many works are several modern Gothic novels, including *A Bloodsmoor Romance* (1982) and *Mysteries of Winterthurn* (1984). She is currently Roger S. Berlind Distinguished Professor at Princeton University. In this extract, Oates compares *The Sun Also Rises* with Fitzgerald's *The Great Gatsby,* noting also the novel's homoerotic overtones and its intensely masculine vision.]

It seems not to be generally recognized that Hemingway's classic novel owes a good deal to F. Scott Fitzgerald's *The Great Gatsby,* which Hemingway read in 1925, after having made Fitzgerald's acquaintance, and admired greatly. Each novel is narrated by a disaffected young man who observes but does not participate centrally in the action; each novel traces the quixotic love of an outsider for a beautiful if infantile woman; each is an excoriation from within of the "lost generation" and the "fiesta concept of life" (Hemingway's phrase)—the aristocratic rich "who give each day the quality of a festival and who, when they have passed and taken the nourishment they need, leave everything dead." Fitzgerald's Daisy is unhappily married to the wealthy Tom Buchanan, whom Gatsby bravely challenges for her love; Hemingway's Brett intends to marry the drunkard wealthy-bankrupt Mike Campbell, whom the hapless

Robert Cohn fights with his fists. (Cohn knocks the inebriated Campbell down but loses Brett, at least temporarily, to a nineteen-year-old bullfighter.) In each novel men and women set themselves the task of being entertained, absorbed, diverted, not by work (though Jake Barnes is a newspaper man of a literary sort) but primarily by drinking and talking. Hemingway's people in particular are obsessed with various forms of sport—golfing, tennis, swimming, hiking, trout fishing, attending boxing matches and bullfights. And drinking. Only in Malcolm Lowry's *Under the Volcano* are drinks so rigorously catalogued, described: whiskey, brandy, champagne, wines of various kinds, absinthe, liqueurs. Long passages are devoted to the correct use of the wine bag in the Spanish Basque region: the drinker should hold the bag at arm's length, then squeeze it so that a long stream of wine "hisses" into the back of the mouth. After a long drunken sequence Jake thinks, "Under the wine I lost the disgusted feeling and was happy. It seemed they were all such nice people."

As a story, *The Sun Also Rises* depends primarily upon the reader's acceptance of Jake Barnes as an intelligent and reliable observer; and of Brett in the role of a thirty-four-year-old Circe awash in alcohol and cheery despair. Though based, like many of Hemingway's characters, on a real person (Lady Duff Twysden, a "legend" in Montparnasse during the time Hemingway and his first wife, Hadley, lived there), Brett is sketchily portrayed: she is "nice," "damned nice," "lovely," "of a very good family," "built with curves like the hull of a racing yacht," but the reader has difficulty envisioning her; Hemingway gives her so little to say that we cannot come to know her as a person. (Whereas Duff Twysden was evidently an artist of some talent and seems to have been an unusually vivacious and intelligent woman.) Another problematic character is the Jew Robert Cohn, who evokes everyone's scorn by "behaving badly"—he follows Brett around and intrudes where he isn't wanted. Cohn is so much the scapegoat for the others' cruelty ("That kike!" "Isn't he awful!" "Was I rude enough to him?" "He doesn't add much to the gaiety," "He has a wonderful quality of bringing out the worst in anybody") that most readers will end up feeling sympathy for him. The fact that Cohn cannot drink as heavily as the others, that the bullfight sickens him (especially the disemboweling of the picador's horse), that in this noisy macho milieu he finally breaks down and cries—these things seem altogether to his credit; he emerges as the novel's most distinctly drawn character. One waits in vain, however, for Jake Barnes to rise to Nick Carraway's judgment of Jay Gatsby: "You're worth the whole damn bunch put together."

The Sun Also Rises is a novel of manners and a homoerotic (though not homosexual) romance, merely in outline a "love story" of unconsummated passion. Like most of Hemingway's books, fiction and nonfiction, it celebrates the mysterious bonds of masculine friendship, sometimes ritualized and sometimes spontaneous; women are viewed with suspicion and an exaggerated awe that turns with mythic ease to contempt. Jake is happiest when he and his friend Bill are away from the company of women altogether and fishing alone in the Rio de la Fabrica valley in Spain. There they achieve a degree of intimacy impossible elsewhere. ("Listen," says Bill. "You're a hell of a good guy, and I'm fonder of you than anybody on earth. I couldn't tell you that in New York. It'd mean I was a faggot.") Of equal importance with male friendship is the worship of the matador, the master of the bull, the only person (in Hemingway's judgment) to really live his life to the full. *Afición* means passion, and an aficionado is one who feels intense passion for the bullfight. Says Jake, "Somehow it was taken for granted that an American could not have *afición*. He might simulate it or confuse it with excitement, but he could not really have it. When they saw that I had *afición*, and there was no password, no set questions that could bring it out, rather it was a sort of oral spiritual examination . . . there was this same embarrassed putting the hand on the shoulder, or a 'Buen hombre.' But nearly always there was the actual touching." Only at certain rigorously defined moments are men allowed to touch one another, just as, in the ritual of the bullfight (bloody and barbarous to those of us who are not aficionados) the tormented bull and the matador "become one" (in Hemingway's repeated phrase) at the moment of the kill. These are quite clearly sacred rites in Hemingway's private cosmology.

If many men are disturbed by Hemingway's code of ethics— as, surely, many women are disturbed by it—it is because

Hemingway's exaggerated sense of maleness really excludes most men. The less than exemplary bullfighter is jeered in the ring, even if he has been gored; poor Robert Cohn, whose flaw seems to have been to have felt too deeply and too openly, is ridiculed, broken, and finally banished from the clique.

If it seems to us highly unjust that Hemingway's men and women derive their sense of themselves by excluding others and by establishing codes of behavior that enforce these exclusions, it should be recalled that Hemingway prided himself on his ability to write of things as they are, not as they might, or should, be. One can object that he does not rise above his prejudices; he celebrates *afición* where he finds it, in the postwar malaise of the 1920s and in his own enigmatic heart.

—Joyce Carol Oates, "The Hemingway Mystique" (1984), *(Woman) Writer: Occasions and Opportunities* (New York: E. P. Dutton, 1988), pp. 306–9

❖

MIMI REISEL GLADSTEIN ON BRETT ASHLEY AS A DESTRUCTIVE WOMAN

[Mimi Reisel Gladstein is a professor of English at the University of Texas at El Paso and the author of *The Ayn Rand Companion* (1984) and *The Indestructible Woman in Faulkner, Hemingway, and Steinbeck* (1986), from which the following extract is taken. Here, Gladstein sees in Brett Ashley a prototype of Hemingway's destructive women.]

Lady Brett Ashley is perhaps one of Hemingway's most attractive destructive women. Her androgynous appearance heightens rather than detracts from her sex appeal. Though she wears her hair like a man's, her figure is described as having "curves like the hull of a racing yacht," and as Jake Barnes notes, she accentuates those curves by wearing a wool jersey. She does not want to adopt a traditionally feminine hairdo and remarks cryptically to Jake that one of the things wrong with her relationship with Pedro Romero was that he wanted her to grow her hair long. "He wanted me to grow my hair out. Me, with long hair. I'd look so like hell." Not only does Brett wear her hair in a boyish bob, but she also dresses in mannish clothing. She wears a "man's felt hat" and "a slipover jersey sweater and a tweed skirt." Her bisexual image is also suggested by her first appearance in the novel. She walks into the scene with a group of her homosexual friends. Jake describes them first. They too are wearing jerseys. "With them was Brett. She looked very lovely and she was very much with them." The suggestion here is that she is very much part of this group, who are men and yet, in Jake's description, mince and gesture in parodies of femininity, masculine and feminine at the same time. Another of Brett's characteristics which acts to blur sexual distinctions is her habit of calling herself "chap." She calls men chaps—"Hello, you chaps"—and then she calls herself the same in ordering a drink—"I say, give a chap a brandy and soda."

The men in her life serve her in much the same manner as religious prostitutes served Aphrodite. First they worship at her shrine; then they prostitute themselves. Jake expresses his adoration of Brett early in the story, telling her he loves her, begging her to live with him. Afterwards, he acts the pimp for her when he sets her up with Pedro Romero. Robert Cohn calls him just that. What is worse, he corrupts his *afición*; that is to say, he prostitutes his passion in order to serve hers. The price is high. At one time he had been acknowledged as one who possessed true *afición*: "When they saw that I had *afición,* and there was no password, no set questions that could bring it out, rather a sort of oral spiritual examination. . . . At once he [they] forgave me all my friends." Jake's clout with Montoya, the high priest of the bull cult, has been strong. When Jake prostitutes his *afición* by introducing Pedro Romero to the kind of woman who will, in the eyes of *aficionados,* ruin him, Montoya will not even nod at Jake. When Jake leaves the hotel, Montoya does not come near him.

But Jake is not the only supplicant for the goddess's favor; more than one of her acolytes prostitutes himself for her. Robert Cohn, in the tradition of giving oneself to a stranger, offers himself to Brett, who is little more than a stranger to him. Once their weekend at San Sebastian is over, she rejects his attempts to give their relationship any special significance. His slavish devotion to her and doglike worship destroy his pride, earn him the animosity of the group, and leave him nothing. In his own words, "I've been through such hell, Jake. Now everything's gone. Everything." The final memento he has to carry away from his encounter with Brett is a sock in the face from Pedro Romero.

Mike Campbell is another of the men who is reduced by his association with Brett while she is affected minimally. Not much can be said for Mike's character to begin with, but it is not enhanced by his association with Brett. At the end of the book he has been "cuckolded" in a sense and left alone and penniless. In fact, he is put in the position of a kept man as Brett puts up most of the money that he gives Montoya to pay their bill in Pamplona. Mike's complete degradation is shown in his final scene with Bill Gorton and Jake Barnes when he commits the unpardonable sin of gambling without money to back his bet. He has spent the last bit of money he has buying drinks and giving extravagant tips to the bartender. His complete lack of character is explored by Bill Gorton as he establishes the fact that Mike not only did not have the money to gamble with, but that he has taken all of Brett's money and still intends to sponge off yet another acquaintance when they drop him off.

Brett's role as a goddess to be worshipped is underscored in the scene with the *riau-riau* dancers. "Brett wanted to dance but they did not want her to. They wanted her as an image to dance around." Robert Cohn articulates her fatal attraction for men. " 'He calls her Circe,' Mike said. 'He claims she turns men into swine.' " Figuratively she does just that. She calls Mike a swine for the way he treats Robert Cohn, responding to Jake's defense of Mike by saying, "Yes. But he didn't need to be a swine." Cohn's behavior is also swinish, as he follows Brett around, sniveling and squealing.

But Brett is not pure bitch-goddess. Certain aspects of her positive mothering qualities are also stressed. She had been a nurse during the war. She and Jake met in a hospital. She "nurses" Romero after his fistfight with Cohn. Mike Campbell comments about her mothering qualities, "She loves looking after people. That's how we came to go off together. She was looking after me." Her mothering role is underscored as she tries to maintain harmony in the group, placating the rivalrous siblings. She chides Mike when he is ugly to Cohn. Her effect on the men is analogous to the effect a strong mother has on her sons. Those who do not exert their independence and kill the domination of the Terrible Mother remain tied to her, thereby abdicating their manhood. Those who are strong, like Romero, who maintain their independence and their principles, are set free. Brett's choice to set Romero free is significant here. She chooses to leave him because she knows she is not good for him. In her depiction of her choice she stresses the difference in their ages. "I'm thirty-four, you know. I'm not going to be one of those bitches that ruins children."

—Mimi Reisel Gladstein, *The Indestructible Woman in Faulkner, Hemingway, and Steinbeck* (Ann Arbor, MI: UMI Research Press, 1986), pp. 59–61

❖

MICHAEL S. REYNOLDS ON *THE SUN ALSO RISES* AS A PERIOD PIECE

[Michael S. Reynolds (b. 1937), a professor of English at North Carolina State University, is the author of *Young Hemingway* (1986) and *Hemingway: The Paris Years* (1989). In this extract, Reynolds notes that *The Sun Also Rises* is a period piece that must be studied in the context of its time.]

More than half a century has now passed since we saw the first light of Hemingway's *The Sun Also Rises*—a half century of bloody war and remarkable change: the jet age, the atomic age, the computer age. Next summer at Pamplona the grandchildren of the twenties will make the pilgrimage, looking under the Irunia arcade for an experience trapped in time. In Paris they will sip their beers under the red and gold awnings of the Dome, imagining faces long since gone under the earth. Great books have a way of doing that to us, a way of stopping time. Nostalgia is infectious and easily forgiven. But critics should know better. The places and the weather may look the same, but all else has changed. The music has changed. The clothes have changed. The prices, the moods, the politics, the values—all irrevocably changed. Brett Ashley and Jake Barnes are no longer our contemporaries. Hemingway, as he said of Henry James, is as dead as he will ever be; to continue to read his first novel as if it were written for our age is to be hopelessly romantic.

The Sun's timeless quality, of course, encourages such behavior, but to persist at it past the point of diminished returns is to devalue the novel. *The Sun Also Rises* is a period piece, a historical artifact as precisely dated as that frozen moment at Pompeii. The year is 1925 as it was in another country. The book could not have been written any earlier, for the Great War had not yet produced the war-wounded generation that peoples *The Sun*. A decade later it would not have been written; in the middle of the Great Depression, no one was interested in boozy expatriates. We can no more properly read *The Sun Also Rises* outside of its social and historical context than we can view Picasso's "Les Demoiselles d'Avignon" as if it were painted last year. Both are works of art anchored in time. To treat either artist as if he were our contemporary is to pretend that we are living in an earlier age. Foolishness, utterly. Our time is not their time. Historically blind readers see only the timeless qualities of the work, and even those they are reading at a discount.

Unfortunately, Hemingway's roman à clef has suffered from one kind of historical context that has severely blurred the novel's true focus. Basing several of the characters, as he did, on real people, Hemingway encouraged readers and critics to waste inordinate effort documenting the parallels. While Hemingway was revising his first draft of *The Sun,* he told Ernest Walsh:

> I believe that when you are writing stories about actual people, not the best thing to do, you should make them those people in everything except telephone addresses. Think that is the only justification for writing stories about actual people.

Some of the earliest reviewers, wanting to dismiss *The Sun* as a trashy novel, picked on this element. The *New York World* said:

For those who know the stamping ground of the American expatriates in Paris—that district clustered about the corner where the Boulevard Raspail crosses the Boulevard Montparnasse—it will become speedily patent that practically all of these characters are directly based on actual people.

The biographical reading of the novel continued until the real characters—Duff Twysden, Pat Guthrie, Harold Loeb, Niño de la Palma—became as familiar as their fictional avatars—Brett, Mike, Cohn, and Pedro Romero. Today the prototypes are all dead, and the reader no longer cares if Duff went to San Sebastian with Loeb or slept with Niño. There remains, however, the tendency to see Jake Barnes as a thinly veiled version of Hemingway himself. To take two steps into that literary bog is to become mired in fictional biography, which is not only factually false but which also says precious little about the novel itself.
—Michael S. Reynolds, "The *Sun* in Its Time: Recovering the Historical Context," *New Essays on* The Sun Also Rises, ed. Linda Wagner-Martin (Cambridge: Cambridge University Press, 1987), pp. 43–44

❖

WILLIAM BALASSI ON THE WRITING OF *THE SUN ALSO RISES*

[William Balassi is the coeditor of *This Is About Vision: Interviews with Southwestern Writers* (1990). In this extract, Balassi studies Hemingway's work on the writing and revision of *The Sun Also Rises*, showing how the elimination of a section at the beginning significantly altered the novel's thrust.]

Hemingway had written the novel in eight and a half weeks, and he was exhausted. "Tired as hell inside," he was, like Jake, drinking a great deal and needed to get away. The following weekend he went to Chartres to unwind, but he could not stop. Instead he wrote a foreword to his novel, which during the previous week he had decided to call "The Lost

Generation," a phrase that ultimately became the book's epigraph. In this foreword he explains that he got the title from Gertrude Stein. One day, when a young, capable mechanic fixed her car, Stein had expressed surprise because she thought that World War I had rendered a whole generation incapable of doing anything well. The garage owner told her that those too young to have fought in the war were fine; rather, "it is the ones between twenty two and thirty that are no good. C'est un generation [*sic*] perdu." It is within this "lost generation" that Hemingway placed himself:

> This is about something that is already finished. For whatever is going to happen to the generation of which I am a part has already happened. . . . There will be more entanglements, there will be more complications, there will be successes and failures. . . . [A few will learn to live perhaps. One or two may learn to write or to paint. . . .] But none of it will matter particularly to this generation because to them the things that are given to people to happen have already happened.

This foreword belies Hemingway's later statement that the Gertrude Stein epigraph was "splendid bombast," and it indicates that he took the "lost generation" phrase seriously. But perhaps because he did not want to be indebted to Stein, Hemingway decided against using it as his title. He then considered other titles: "The Sun Also Rises," "Rivers to the Sea," "Two Lie Together," and "The Old Leaven." The fact that all of these quotations come from the Bible suggests that Hemingway intended to use his title to point to the religious dimensions of this apparently secular novel.

After the weekend in Chartres Hemingway put aside the manuscript for several months. Then in late November or early December he started to revise it. Three times he tried to rework the original opening—twice as a third-person narration—but the task of reconciling the details of the opening story with those of the novel was proving difficult, and he eventually decided to begin instead with the portrait of Duff.

This change from *in medias res* to straight chronology altered the novel in a fundamental way. Hemingway had written the manuscript assuming that he did not have to explain things, as the reader already knew about Pamplona. But eliminating the beginning story removed the referent for much that followed. In effect Hemingway had created a different kind of *in medias res,* one that starts not in the middle of the plot, but in the middle of the text. This transformed the text into an impressive—if unplanned-for—example of his iceberg theory of writing. The year before he had done the same thing with "Indian Camp" when he cut the beginning because it explained too much about young Nick Adams. Without the opening scene in Pamplona, the reader has to sense the importance of lines that have lost their context, to sense more than he knows, which is possible because the text appropriates and internalizes the significance of the opening material while omitting the story itself. The omission of this story also creates a compelling sense of inevitability about events in the novel, an inextricable movement toward *something.* The reader experiences the relentless working out of events already set in motion long before the fiesta. Eliminating the opening story transformed the novel into a tragedy, and the Paris section, originally intended as background to help the reader "understand what happened in Pamplona," now sets the tragic forces into motion. ⟨. . . ⟩

Hemingway had written a tightly constructed, multileveled, and masterfully understated novel. It was a remarkable achievement, especially for a first novel. He had started with actual people who came with fully equipped personalities. This helped him create complex yet consistent characters, because what he wrote in the opening story had to ring true with what he knew; and later it helped him project a fiction that was as "true" as anything he had taken from actuality. He had good material to work with: an exotic festival, a fascinating mix of characters, a volatile emotional situation, and his own painful and intense emotions. He wrote with skill and exuberance, the young artist realizing his potential, playing with form and technique day by day. He took chances. He daringly left things out as he wrote. He deleted explanatory and speculative passages. He refused to interpret for the reader, presenting scenes without comment, offering minimal descriptions, and pointing to embedded symbols and clues only obscurely. And in revision he transformed the novel into a tragedy. By the time he was done, Hemingway emerged with a large, complex but tightly

compressed story that more than sixty years after its publication we are still learning how to read.

—William Balassi, "Hemingway's Greatest Iceberg: The
Composition of *The Sun Also Rises,*" *Writing the American
Classics,* ed. James Barbour and Tom Quirk (Chapel Hill:
University of Nebraska Press, 1990), pp. 146–48, 150

❖

NANCY R. COMLEY AND ROBERT SCHOLES ON GENDER ROLES
IN *THE SUN ALSO RISES*

[Nancy R. Comley is a professor of English at Queens
College of the City University of New York and the
coeditor of *Writing and Reading Differently* (1985).
Robert Scholes, a professor of English at Brown University, is a leading literary critic and theorist. Among his
books are *Structuralism in Literature: An Introduction*
(1974), *Fabulation and Metafiction* (1979), and *Textual
Power* (1985). In this extract from *Hemingway's
Genders* (1994), Comley and Scholes study the complex interplay of gender roles in *The Sun Also Rises.*]

The action of *The Sun Also Rises* opens with Jake Barnes picking up a Paris prostitute, his companion for the evening. This
serves as the outer frame for the introduction of Brett; the inner
frame is of bitchy dinner conversation and the actual introduction of Brett as the centerpiece in a garland of gay young men.
The framing alerts us to read Brett in terms of both a bitchiness
and a sexuality that are different from what might be considered normal for women of her position. Not that she is to be
seen as representing bitchiness, prostitution, or homosexuality
but that she should be seen in relation to these concepts. Like
her gypsy prototype, Carmen, Brett is "unfeminine" in her
usurping of the male prerogative of promiscuity on her own
terms. And the question of whether or not she is a bitch is, in
her own view and in that of the text in which she is represented,
the central ethical issue of her life. Brett first appears in *The Sun*

Also Rises entering a dance club while surrounded by homosexual men, a crowd with whom "one can drink in such safety," as she puts it. Jake Barnes has brought his dinner companion, Georgette, a prostitute he will not touch nor allow to touch him: "You sick?" she asks, and when he says he is, she replies, "Everybody's sick. I'm sick, too." Georgette is swept off to the dance floor by the homosexuals, who are happy to dance with her. Jake, who dislikes them, sees them synechdochically, as fragments of men: "I could see their hands and newly washed, wavy hair in the light from the door. . . . As they went in, under the light I saw white hands, wavy hair, white faces, grimacing, gesturing, talking." Disliking their bodies, Jake disembodies them: "Somehow they made me angry. I know they are supposed to be amusing, and you should be tolerant, but I wanted to swing on one, any one, anything to shatter that superior, simpering composure."

Why such anger? Perhaps because the homosexuals are built like "normal" men yet (Jake might think) do not choose to be "normal," while Jake, who has a "normal" male's sex drive, has been left only fragments of sexual apparatus. He cannot perform, though he desires to do so, while the homosexuals can perform and yet do not desire "normal" heterosexual sex. The sexually fragmented Jake is thus linked to men he perceives in fragments as unmanly because he has himself been unmanned. Indeed, his wound has put him in the passive feminine position of lack and has put Brett in the active position of finding men to provide the apparatus that Jake has lost. Although Brett can maintain a kind of objectivity about her sexual engagements, she suffers from being in love with Jake; while he may find being in love "enjoyable," Brett thinks "it's hell on earth." Yet she must see Jake, and however painful that must be for her, she is willing to pay the price for it. In this novel, the insiders are those who pay their own way and who know the values. While Jake is always careful to pay his own way, as the detailing of his financial transactions makes clear, Brett is frequently being bailed out financially. But her lack of ready cash is beside the point, for Brett has paid in other ways and continues to pay emotionally. After a bout of drinking, Jake muses on this aspect of sexual difference: "I thought I had paid for everything. Not like the woman who pays and pays and pays. No idea of retribution or punishment."

In the economy of the text Brett goes on paying even while functioning as a highly valued object of desire. The centrality of her position is played out at the height of the fiesta—which is, with its bullfights, an avatar of ancient fertility rites—when Brett is chosen by the garlic-wreathed riau-riau dancers as "an image to dance around." She functions here as an unlikely vestal virgin in these ancient rites, and she succumbs to their power, as exemplified by Pedro Romero, the handsome young bullfighter whom she perceives as the phallus personified. Irresistibly drawn to him, she enlists Jake's aid in this sexual affair. "I don't say it's right. It is right though for me. God knows, I've never felt such a bitch." Romero is drawn to her as well, and he wants to marry her and make her "more womanly" by having her hair grow out. She eventually leaves Romero because she knows that she will be bad for him: "I'm not going to be one of those bitches that ruins children." She has no religion and not much money, but Brett does have a code of ethics; having partially recovered from her affair with Romero, she tells Jake, "You know it makes one feel rather good deciding not to be a bitch. . . . It's sort of what we have instead of God." As her earlier statement indicates, Brett has demythologized Romero from the perfect phallus to the very young man that he is. She thus gives up a lover of physical and moral perfection for men who are less than perfect but more her "sort of thing."

In Brett's manner of giving up Romero, Hemingway has allotted her a moment of maternal feeling that mitigates her masculine image as a Carmen who loves and leaves whomever she pleases. At the same time, by presenting her as consciously deciding not to be a bitch, Hemingway moves her away from that version of female excess—bitchiness—toward a more manly resignation. What makes Brett interesting as a character is the way that Hemingway has assigned her qualities from both sides of his gendered repertory of typical figures and situated her somewhere between the extremes of good and bad behavior on both scales.
—Nancy R. Comley and Robert Scholes, *Hemingway's Genders: Rereading the Hemingway Text* (New Haven: Yale University Press, 1994), pp. 43–46

❖

[Linda Patterson Miller is a professor of English at Pennsylvania State University (Ogontz Campus). In this extract, Miller finds that the denigrating remarks of many critics on Brett Ashley are symptomatic of the abuse that many beautiful women must face because of their appearance.]

Since the publication of Ernest Hemingway's *The Sun Also Rises* in 1926, readers and critics have derogated Brett Ashley as Hemingway's ultimate bitch. Whether labeling her as a drunkard, a nymphomaniac, or a modern-day Circe who turns men into swine, these interpretations ignore the complexity of Brett's character and the intricate role she plays in the novel, particularly with regard to her stunning beauty. "Take Brett out" of the novel, says critic Harold Bloom, "and vitality would depart." He adds that only when the critic puts aside "the vision of Hemingway's heroine as a Circe" will he discover "there is more inwardness to Lady Brett." That most critics have not yet seen beyond that "vision" helps to illustrate Brett's dilemma as a beautiful woman whose appearance both identifies and traps her.

Hemingway gives few specific details about Brett's physical appearance. She looks "quite beautiful" in a "black, sleeveless evening dress" during a dinner at Pamplona, and, on another occasion, she wears a wool jersey that accentuates the curves of her body "like the hull of a racing yacht." For the most part, she seems to have adopted the natural look, going bare-legged in Paris and brushing her hair back like a boy's (when she is not hiding it under a hat). Besides Jake's statement that Brett is "damned good-looking," and his repeated assertions that Brett looks lovely, or Brett's own admission that she has the "wrong type" of face for a "religious atmosphere," her stark and unconventional beauty becomes known primarily through reactions to her.

Wherever Brett goes, both men and women notice her. When she walks through the streets of Pamplona with Jake, several women come to a wineshop window to watch Brett pass. Robert Cohn, when he first sees Brett, stares dumbfounded. His look of "deserving expectation" (much as "his compatriot must have looked when he saw the promised land") typifies the response that Brett evokes from others, particularly men. As Roger Whitlow notes, "every significant male character in the novel at one time or another comments on Brett's female attractiveness." The fiesta scene, in which chanting men dance around Brett, best illuminates her dilemma as a woman known primarily for her beauty. As Jake tells it, they want her "as an image to dance around." They do not want her.

Trapped within a superficial and misleading image determined for her by others, Brett Ashley feels increasingly isolated, which Jake recognizes when he says that Brett "can't go anywhere alone." She fears being alone precisely because she is alone, more so than any other character in the novel. Because Jake understands her entrapment and isolation, she relies upon him in her struggle to break free of the image that both defines and smothers her.

When Robert Cohn, having just met Brett, comments that she is remarkably attractive and that "she seems to be absolutely fine and straight," Jake tries to counter Cohn's idealism and his presumptuous assertions. "She's a drunk," Jake tells Cohn. "You talk sort of bitter," Cohn replies defensively. "Sorry. I didn't mean to. I was just trying to give you the facts." Throughout the conversation with Cohn, Jake reveals his understanding that as men idealize Brett, falling in love with their image of her rather than with the real person (complete with human foibles), they progressively undermine her sense of self. Jake emphasizes to Cohn that while "her name's Lady Ashley," "Brett's her own name." To a great extent, the novel revolves around Brett's nascent assertiveness and self-awareness as she struggles to realize, finally, "her own name." As Jake narrates Brett's story, he uses parallel structures and mirroring devices that reveal Brett within a larger emotional framework and emphasize the fact that appearances can both deceive and destroy.

—Linda Patterson Miller, "Brett Ashley: The Beauty of It All," *Critical Essays on Ernest Hemingway's* The Sun Also Rises, ed. James Nagel (New York: G. K. Hall, 1995), pp. 170–71

❖

Books by
Ernest Hemingway

Three Stories & Ten Poems. 1923.

in our time. 1924.

In Our Time: Stories. 1925.

The Torrents of Spring: A Romantic Novel in Honor of the Passing of a Great Race. 1926.

Today Is Friday. 1926.

The Sun Also Rises. 1926.

Men without Women. 1927.

A Farewell to Arms. 1929.

Death in the Afternoon. 1932.

God Rest You Merry Gentlemen. 1933.

Winner Take Nothing. 1933.

Green Hills of Africa. 1935.

To Have and Have Not. 1937.

The Spanish Earth. 1938.

The Fifth Column and the First Forty-nine Stories. 1938.

For Whom the Bell Tolls. 1940.

Men at War: The Best War Stories of All Time (editor). 1942.

Voyage to Victory: An Eye-witness Report of the Battle for a Normandy Beachhead. 1944.

The Portable Hemingway. Ed. Malcolm Cowley. 1944.

Selected Short Stories. c. 1945.

The Essential Hemingway. 1947.

Across the River and into the Trees. 1950.

The Old Man and the Sea. 1952.

The Hemingway Reader. Ed. Charles Poore. 1953.

Two Christmas Tales. 1959.

Collected Poems. 1960.

The Snows of Kilimanjaro and Other Stories. 1961.

The Wild Years. Ed. Gene Z. Hanrahan. 1962.

A Moveable Feast. 1964.

By-Line: Ernest Hemingway: Selected Articles and Dispatches of Four Decades. Ed. William White. 1967.

The Fifth Column and Four Stories of the Spanish Civil War. 1969.

Ernest Hemingway, Cub Reporter. Ed. Matthew J. Bruccoli. 1970.

Islands in the Stream. 1970.

Ernest Hemingway's Apprenticeship: Oak Park 1916–1917. Ed. Matthew J. Bruccoli. 1971.

The Nick Adams Stories. 1972.

88 Poems. Ed. Nicholas Gerogiannis. 1979, 1992 (as *Complete Poems*).

Selected Letters 1917–1961. Ed. Carlos Baker. 1981.

The Dangerous Summer. 1985.

Dateline, Toronto: Hemingway's Complete Toronto Star *Dispatches, 1920–1924.* Ed. William White. 1985.

The Garden of Eden. 1986.

Complete Short Stories. 1987.

Remembering Spain: Hemingway's Civil War Eulogy and the Veterans of the Abraham Lincoln Brigade. Ed. Cary Nelson. 1994.

Works about
Ernest Hemingway and
The Sun Also Rises

Adams, Richard P. "Sunrise out of *The Waste Land.*" *Tulane Studies in English* 9 (1959): 119–31.

Balassi, William. "The Trail to *The Sun Also Rises:* The First Week of Writing." In *Hemingway: Essays of Reassessment,* ed. Frank Scafella. New York: Oxford University Press, 1991, pp. 33–51.

Baldwin, Marc D. "Class Consciousness and the Ideology of Dominance in *The Sun Also Rises.*" *McNeese Review* 33 (1990–94): 14–33.

Barnett, Louise K. "The Dialectic of Discourse in *The Sun Also Rises.*" *University of Mississippi Studies in English* 8 (1990): 168–84.

Bloom, Harold, ed. *Brett Ashley.* New York: Chelsea House, 1991.

———, ed. *Ernest Hemingway's* The Sun Also Rises. New York: Chelsea House, 1987.

Brenner, Gerry. "A 'Vulgar' Ethic: *The Sun Also Rises.*" In Brenner's *Concealments in Hemingway's Works.* Columbus: Ohio State University Press, 1983, pp. 42–61.

Budick, Emily Miller. "*The Sun Also Rises:* Hemingway's New Covenant of History." In Budick's *Fiction and Historical Consciousness: The American Romance Tradition.* New Haven: Yale University Press, 1989, pp. 164–84.

Casillo, Robert. "The Festival Gone Wrong: Vanity and Victimization in *The Sun Also Rises.*" *Essays in Literature* 13 (1986): 115–33.

Cohen, Milton A. "Circe and Her Swine: Domination and Debasement in *The Sun Also Rises.*" *Arizona Quarterly* 41 (1985): 293–305.

Cooper, Stephen. *The Politics of Ernest Hemingway.* Ann Arbor, MI: UMI Research Press, 1987.

Curtis, Mary Ann. "*The Sun Also Rises:* Its Relation to *The Song of Roland.*" *American Literature* 60 (1988): 274–77.

Grenberg, Bruce L. "The Design of Heroism in *The Sun Also Rises.*" *Fitzgerald/Hemingway Annual,* 1971, pp. 247–89.

Hays, Peter L. *Ernest Hemingway.* New York: Ungar, 1990.

Helbig, Doris A. "Confession, Clarity, and Community in *The Sun Also Rises.*" *South Atlantic Review* 58 (1993): 85–110.

Hemingway Review 6, No. 1 (Fall 1986). Special *The Sun Also Rises* issue.

Hinkle, James. "Some Unexpected Sources for *The Sun Also Rises.*" *Hemingway Review* 2, No. 1 (1982): 26–42.

Kert, Bernice. *The Hemingway Women.* New York: Norton, 1983.

Lewis, Robert W. *Hemingway on Love.* Austin: University of Texas Press, 1965.

Lockridge, Ernest. " 'Primitive Emotions': A Tragedy of Revenge Called *The Sun Also Rises.*" *Journal of Narrative Technique* 20 (1990): 42–55.

Lynn, Kenneth S. *Hemingway.* New York: Simon & Schuster, 1987.

Lynn, David H. *The Hero's Tale: Narrators in the Early Modern Novel.* New York: St. Martin's Press, 1989.

Merrill, Robert. "Demoting Hemingway." *American Literature* 60 (1988): 255–68.

Messent, Peter B. *Ernest Hemingway.* New York: St. Martin's Press, 1992.

Morgan, Kathleen. "Between Two Worlds: Hemingway's Brett Ashley and Homer's Helen of Troy." *Classical and Modern Literature* 11 (1991): 169–80.

Morrow, Patrick D. "The Bought Generation: Another Look at Money in *The Sun Also Rises.*" *Genre* 13 (1980): 51–69.

Reynolds, Michael S. The Sun Also Rises: *A Novel of the Twenties.* Boston: Twayne, 1988.

Rosen, Kenneth B., ed. *Hemingway Repossessed.* Westport, CT: Praeger, 1994.

Ross, Morton L. "Bill Gorton, the Preacher in *The Sun Also Rises.*" *Modern Fiction Studies* 18 (1972): 517–27.

Rovit, Earl, and Gerry Brenner. *Ernest Hemingway.* 2nd ed. Boston: Twayne, 1986.

Rudat, Wolfgang E. H. *Alchemy in* The Sun Also Rises: *Hidden Gold in Hemingway's Narrative.* Lewiston, NY: Edwin Mellen Press, 1992.

———. *A Rotten Way to Be Wounded: The Tragicomedy of* The Sun Also Rises. New York: Peter Lang, 1990.

Sarason, Bertram D., ed. *Hemingway and the* Sun *Set.* Washington, DC: NCR Microcard Editions, 1972.

Spilka, Mark. *Hemingway's Quarrel with Androgyny.* Lincoln: University of Nebraska Press, 1990.

Stallman, R. W. "*The Sun Also Rises*—But No Bells Ringing." In Stallman's *The Houses That James Built and Other Literary Studies.* East Lansing: Michigan State University Press, 1961, pp. 173–93.

Steinke, Jim. "Brett and Jake in Spain: Hemingway's Ending for *The Sun Also Rises.*" *Spectrum* 27 (1985): 131–41.

Strychacz, Thomas. "Dramatizations of Manhood in Hemingway's *In Our Time* and *The Sun Also Rises.*" *American Literature* 61 (1989): 245–60.

Svoboda, Frederic Joseph. *Hemingway and* The Sun Also Rises: *The Crafting of a Style.* Lawrence: University Press of Kansas, 1983.

Thorn, Lee. "*The Sun Also Rises:* Good Manners Make Good Art." *Hemingway Review* 8, No. 1 (Fall 1988): 42–49.

Torchiana, Donald T. "*The Sun Also Rises:* A Reconsideration." *Fitzgerald/Hemingway Annual,* 1969, pp. 77–103.

Wedin, Warren. "Trout Fishing and Self-Betrayal in *The Sun Also Rises.*" *Arizona Quarterly* 37 (1981): 63–74.

Whitlow, Roger. *Cassandra's Daughters: The Women in Hemingway.* Westport, CT: Greenwood Press, 1984.

Williams, Wirt. *The Tragic Art of Ernest Hemingway.* Baton Rouge: Louisiana State University Press, 1981, pp. 40–64.

Young, Philip. *Ernest Hemingway: A Reconsideration.* University Park: Pennsylvania State University Press, 1966.

Index of
Themes and Ideas

FIESTA, and its role in the novel, 16–20, 28, 34, 39, 50, 55, 63, 65

GORTON, BILL, and his role in the novel, 12–20, 39, 47, 52, 55

GRACE UNDER PRESSURE, as theme, 19–20, 22, 23

GREAT GATSBY, THE (Fitzgerald), and how it compares, 5, 40–53

HEMINGWAY, ERNEST: as hard-boiled, 27; "iceberg theory" of, 59–60; life of, 7–9; style of, 32–33, 42

HONOR, as theme, 28

IN OUR TIME, and how it compares, 25–27, 28

LIGHT, as symbol, 41–42

MIPPIPOPOLOUS, COUNT, and his role in the novel, 11, 12, 38, 39, 40–41, 46–47

MONTOYA, and his role in the novel, 15, 17, 54

MORALITY, as theme, 13, 15, 21, 27–29, 31–33

ODYSSEY, THE (Homer), and how it compares, 34

ROMERO, PEDRO: Brett's affair with, 17–23, 31, 37, 44–45, 49, 51, 54–56, 63; Cohn's fight with, 19–20, 22, 23, 37, 38, 55; as Hemingway hero, 19, 23, 32, 58; and his role in the novel, 17–23, 42

SELF-CONTROL, as theme, 36–37, 46, 47–50

STOICISM, as theme, 42–43, 49–50

SUN ALSO RISES, THE: allegorical figures in, 42–43; anti-Semitism of, 10, 12; as autobiography, 48–49, 58; composition of, 25, 57, 58–61; dialogue in, 46–47; drinking in, 14, 34, 46–47, 51; as elegy, 5–6; emotional pattern of, 40–42; epigraphs to, 6, 10–11, 14, 27, 49, 59; fishing episode in, 14, 29, 52; Fitzgerald on, 24; flaws of, 24, 27, 38–39; forward to, 59; gender roles in, 61–63; historical basis for characters in, 51, 58; homoeroticism of, 50–53; and lost generation, 39–42, 50, 59; masculine vision of, 50–53; natural knowledge in, 34–35; nihilism of, 6; opening of, 10, 58–61; oppressiveness of, 29; as period piece, 38–39, 56–58; as prose-poem, 5; purpose of, 24–25; romanticism in, 47–50; as tragedy, 25, 29, 60; unrealistic characters in, 27, 29–30, 41; verbosity of, 24; and World War I, 37–39, 42–43

WASTE LAND, THE (Eliot), and how it compares, 5, 33–35, 40, 42, 48